THE WILD WHEEL

Garet Garrett

PANTHEON BOOKS, NEW YORK

First Printing
February, 1952

The author and publishers express herewith their
thanks to the Free Library, Philadelphia (Automo-
tive Collection), the Ford Motor Company, Dearborn
and New York, and Wide World Photos Inc., New
York, for kind permission to reproduce photographs
from their collections.

MANUFACTURED IN THE UNITED STATES
BY KINGSPORT PRESS, INC., KINGSPORT, TENNESSEE
DESIGNED BY ANDOR BRAUN

CONTENTS

Laissez faire was a religion that grew to full size in the American environment and never anywhere else. It was founded on the doctrine of Adam Smith's unseen hand, the mysterious power of which was to bring it to pass that the individual, freely pursuing his own selfish ends, was nevertheless bound to serve the common good, whether he consciously intended to do so or not, or ever thought about it at all. It was cruel in the way that nature is cruel to weak and marginal things; but it worked. How and why naturally it produced here the most fabulous material achievement in the history of the human race is the subject of many heavy and quarrelsome books in the library of social and economic theory. The idea of this book is to make you see it working through the eyes of its darling practician.

If in this country, for both good and evil, free private enterprise had its logical manifestations in a prodigious manner, so Henry Ford was its extreme and last pure event. After him it was different. The religion

declined. It no longer exists in the orthodox form anywhere.

But this is not a history of Ford and his times, nor
a biography either, furnished with notes, conclusions
and a philosophy of meaning. Rather, it is a structure
of episode, word and deed, like a dwelling, and the man
is there—a kind of divine mechanic, the ultimate child
of his era, acting upon his world with ruthless and terrible energy, by instinct and intuition, who thought
with his hands. As you watch him coming in and going
out you may not understand him. Indeed, it is very
probable that he did not understand himself. But you
will perhaps get some feeling of life and its lusty trans-
actions under the creed of Laissez Faire, and thereby
arrive at a judgment of your own concerning what we
have left behind.

G. G.

ONE

SWEAT IN PARADISE

I t was Sunday. We were making up the forms of "The Annalist" in the composing room of the New York *Times* when Mr. Ochs appeared, threading his way toward us between the turtles. His arms were held a little out, as if he were bearing a load on his chest, and his eyes were wide and staring. By these signs we knew his mind was buzzing. When he spoke it was hardly above a whisper, saying:

"He's crazy, isn't he? Don't you think he has gone crazy?"

We knew what he meant. The news was in the morning paper that the Ford Motor Company had announced a minimum wage of five dollars a day for all employees down to the floor sweepers; the day's work at the same time was cut from nine to eight hours.

The year was 1914. Only those then living at an age of awareness can believe what a sensation that announcement made, not here only but all over the world. Until then the Ford Motor Company had been paying the prevailing wage, which was a little over two dollars a day.

American industry was rocked to its heels. Four kinds of ruin were commonly prophesied. First, Detroit would be ruined by an exodus of employers; second, those who remained and tried to meet the Ford wage scale would go bankrupt; third, the Ford Motor Company itself would fall; fourth, the Ford employees would be demoralized by this sudden affluence; they wouldn't know how to spend the money.

I said to Mr. Ochs: "It might be well to have a look. I'll go out and see."

The barber who shaved me the next morning at the Book-Cadillac in Detroit said: "Our Mr. Ford has gone crazy. Did you know?"

At breakfast four men came to my table to confirm the barber's opinion. They were employers of labor. I asked them if they were going to leave Detroit, and they said they were. Ford could have it.

Meanwhile an event of inverted cruelty was building itself on the Ford hiring lot. When the thing happened, the bitter people of Detroit made the most of it. In near-zero weather, from before dawn until dark, thousands of wistful men were milling about in front of the employment office, which of course was swamped. They came from everywhere. It was tidal migration, rising in the hills and valleys and in other cities, like a gold rush— from the two-dollar day to the five-dollar day. Word went forth that only a few more workers were needed and these would be found in Detroit. That had no effect at all. Every incoming freight train brought more of

10

them, shivering in empty freight cars or clinging to the bumpers, with the light of a five-dollar job in their eyes. No matter how it got there, a motley of ten thousand disappointed and wretched men, standing on the cold side of the door to a wage earner's heaven, would become restive and a little ugly. It obstructed traffic and refused to disperse. Then the police were called in; and what was perhaps the most innocent mob that had ever assembled itself anywhere was scattered by icy streams from the fire hose.

The plant was then at Highland Park. River Rouge came later.

I spent the next two days with Ford. He made it seem quite simple. He said: "If the floor sweeper's heart is in his job he can save us five dollars a day by picking up small tools instead of sweeping them out."

Years later he wrote:

"Unless an industry can so manage itself as to keep wages high and prices low it destroys itself, for otherwise it limits the number of its customers. One's own employees ought to be one's own best customers. The real progress of our company dates from 1914, when we raised the minimum wage from somewhat more than two dollars to a flat five dollars a day, for then we increased the buying power of our own people, and they increased the buying power of other people, and so on and on. It is this thought of enlarging buying power by paying high wages and selling at low prices that is behind the prosperity of this country."

That was in his book *Today and Tomorrow*,* which he did in collaboration with Samuel Crowther in 1926. The complete theory had by that time arrived—the theory, namely, that the wage earner is more important as a consumer than as a producer. How much of that formulation was Ford's and how much of it Crowther's one cannot say. They wrote several books together, with Ford speaking in the first person as *I* or *we*, and the ideas were entirely his own, but as he conceived them they were wordless revelations or sudden flashes of insight. It was Crowther's part to clothe them with reason and argument and house them in proper premises.

Ford knew something about the behavior of his own mind. He would say: "We go forward without the facts." Or: "We learn the facts as we go along."

To which Crowther would add some rhetorical phrases on vision for the pioneer and facts for the plodder.

I once asked Ford where ideas came from. Did he beat them out of his head or stare them out of a blank wall?

There was something like a saucer on the desk in front of him. He flipped it upside down and kept tapping the bottom with his fingers as he said: "You know atmospheric pressure is hitting there at fourteen pounds per square inch. You can't see it and you can't feel it. Yet you know it is happening. It's that way with ideas. The air is full of them. They are knocking you on the

* *Today and Tomorrow,* by Henry Ford. Copyright 1926 by Doubleday & Co., Inc.

head. You don't have to think about it too much. You only have to know what you want. Just suspend in your mind the thought of what it is you want. If you do that, then you can forget it. You can go about your business thinking and talking of other things, and suddenly the idea you want will come through. It was there all the time."

Then one day I saw it work. I was in Cameron's office when Ford came in unexpectedly, just looking around. "You," he said to me, sitting down and putting his feet on the desk, "are just the man I want to see. You are one person I think of who can make this subject of money clear to everybody."

It happened at that time that money was his obsessional diversion. He had but recently induced his bosom friend Thomas A. Edison to invent a new kind of money; the Edison plan, already published, had turned out to be one of the quaint additions to the queer side of monetary literature. Even Ford seemed to know that.

I said: "The trouble is, Mr. Ford, I've learned that I don't know anything about money."

"Good!" he said. "That's why you can do it. The people who write on money all begin with knowing too much about it."

With that he was off in his most voluble manner. What was money? It was holy water. Here was the largest automobile company in the world. Did money do it? Money had nothing to do with it. Here he was, supposed to be one of the very rich men in the world.

13

But look (turning his pockets inside out). He had no money. Yet of course money was necessary as a sign. The use of it was to enable people to exchange things of value. But it ought to be that simple. The bankers had so bitched it up, with their speculations and manipulations, that now nobody could understand it. If only—

And so the monologue went for more than an hour. Cameron wearily looked at the clock and said it was time for lunch. Ford led the way; as we were going through the door Cameron held back a little and muttered to me: "Do you wonder how so much chaff can come out of what you know to be really a fine mill?"

At the lunch table Ford went on, not from where he had been interrupted but from a new beginning, until the soup was served. Then suddenly his tall body stiffened; the expression of his face, which had been very lively, changed to that a sleepwalker, and he said to no one in particular—to himself, really: "A-h-h! I'm not thinking about that at all." With no other word he rose abruptly, kicked back his chair and walked rapidly away. An idea that he had been wanting had come through and he was gone to do something about it.

Cameron said: "That happens often. He won't be back. We may not see him again for a week."

2

THE facts that "came afterward" from the five-dollar day were startling, some in kind and some in degree. That the buying power of the Ford wage earner alone

14

was increased had in itself no social meaning—not then, not until a high-wage policy began to make itself felt as an example throughout American industry. But the immediate effect upon the individual was electric, and this was an effect produced not by five dollars a day in his pocket but by the contrast between the Ford wage and a wage anywhere else. That was what determined the man's attitude toward his job.

During that first visit with Ford we spent most of two days in the plant. That was where he loved to be. He hated the office and was uneasy there. The spectacle of work excited his mind.

I had learned to know the sounds of industry, particularly the difference between the rhythm of a piece-work shop and that of a time-pay shop. The music of manufacture has in each case a certain tempo, and as it crashes on your ear you will remember, if you happen to know it, the chant of the old flax breakers—

B-y . . . t-h-e . . . d-a-y . . . B-y . . . t-h-e . . . d-a-y . . . B-y . . . t-h-e . . . d-a-y.
Bythepiece-Bythepiece-Bythepiece.

Well, here it was all by the day, and yet never had I heard a rhythm so fast in a piece-work shop.

At that time a great deal of material was moved in dolly bins trundled by hand along the floor. A man at the top of a long aisle would start toward us with his bin and come so fast that he couldn't stop short if he wanted to, but he didn't want to stop or slow down and it was Ford who had to leap aside to let him pass. And

15

that was all you had to see. The labor cost of producing an automobile was falling before your eyes because every worker in the place was like the man with the dolly bin. Five years later, when the minimum wage had been increased to six dollars a day, Ford said:

"The payment of five dollars a day for an eight-hour day was one of the finest cost-cutting moves we ever made, and the six-dollar-a-day wage is cheaper than the five. How far this will go we do not know."

The next rise, to seven dollars a day, occurred in 1929, after the great stock market crash, when everybody else was thinking of how to cut wages. This was Ford's dramatic contribution to the hope of immediate recovery; and unhappily it had very little effect. It did not even increase the buying power of Ford workers, because almost immediately the Ford plant had to go on short time.

Two years later, when the whole country was in the slough of despond, I found Ford playing around with his supreme hobby, which was Greenfield Village, as if he had nothing else on his mind.

I said to Cameron: "He thought he had the answer to depression. Now how does he take it?"

Cameron said: "I don't know. He doesn't talk about it much. It's so terrible that I believe he doesn't dare let himself think about it."

For a man who normally had hair-trigger opinions on any subject under the sun, his silence at this time was notable. The reflections to which he gave any expression at all, privately or publicly, were either puerile or grotesquely inadequate. Several times he said it was probably a blessing. Everything that people were saying about it was wrong. He was sure of this because people were always wrong. But that was as far as he could get.

It was a chasm that his mind apparently could not bridge. For years he had been saying: "We need have no slumps in business. We need never have unemployment. Our recipe for hard times is to lower prices and increase wages. And it would take the efforts of only a few large companies thus to check the panic of any depression."

Business, indeed, might have its ups and downs, but they were unimportant because—

"We have attained such speed that slowing down for economic crossings or curves does not mean anything. When the limited passing through crowded sections cuts down from sixty to thirty miles an hour, it does not mean the train is going to stop or even slump. But those who are fearful are always looking out for signs of a slump. Often it would seem that neurasthenics manage business."

And he knew what caused the slowings down. Business was continually putting the profit motive over what he called the wage motive. When business thought only of profit for the owners "instead of providing goods for

17

all," then it frequently broke down—so frequently that scientists had invented what they called "business cycles."

But in those simple terms you could not explain the Great Depression, and even if you thought you could, what good would it do? Merely to increase wages was not the answer. At the onset of the depression he had tried that, with no result whatever.

Moreover, from the first five-dollar day, which was his famous example, there had been a bonanza effect— an effect upon the worker's productivity and therefore upon labor costs—that could not repeat itself. Remember, it was not the five-dollar wage that produced that effect; it was the doubling of wages that did it. As other automobile manufacturers followed his example and adopted his methods, five dollars a day became the prevailing wage in Detroit and the special incentive of the Ford wage was lost. Could he double wages again—to ten dollars? If so, could he double them again to twenty dollars? The productivity of labor could not be increased that fast. The method of increasing it in a marvelous manner, by bringing the work to the man on an assembly line and breaking each man's task down to a few repetitive reflex motions—that method had been discovered once for all. It could no more be discovered again than a gold deposit. It could only be worked harder, perhaps against the law of diminishing returns. In any case, there was no magic in the Ford wage as such; the magic was what he got for the wage he paid.

18

And so it was that Ford, who discovered familiar things with the innocence of first-seeing, discovered that the matter of wages was a very complex matter indeed; and the more he thought about it the more grim he was.

3

HERE the threads of irony begin to appear in the weave. By example and precept and with the authority of success, one man had caused a revolutionary change to begin in ways of thinking about wages and profits and what business was for. On that account both labor and industry owed him an immense debt and both paid it in bad coin. He came to be hated by labor, which found his discipline too hard; and industry could never forgive him for what he did to its complacency.

In the end he was defeated. A new time came. Now Ford workers smoke at their tasks as workers do everywhere else, their unions tell the management how fast they will work and for what wages, and the Ford Motor Company prices its cars as all other automobile makers do. All this he lived to see.

About midway of his experience with a high-wage policy, the minimum by that time having reached six dollars a day, Ford came to this reflection:

"We don't know what the right wage is and perhaps we shall never know. The world has never approached industry with the wage motive—from the angle of seeing how high wages may be—and until it has we shall not know much about wages."

Then he tried this definition:

"The right price is not what the traffic will bear. The right wage is not the lowest sum a man will work for. The right price is the lowest price an article can steadily be sold for. The right wage is the highest wage the employer can steadily pay."

Perfect perhaps as a generalization; and yet it leaves unaccounted for so many variables and so many elements of guess, judgment and hazard that it can hardly be taken as a working rule whereby wages may be determined. For example, what of the profit that comes from better method and engineering, more intense technology, better tools put into the hands of the worker? To whom does that belong? How shall it be divided? Ford said:

"It is not long since the emphasis in industry was on profit for the owner. The emphasis now is on profit for the wage earner. The narrow capitalist and the narrow trade unionist have exactly the same point of view. They differ only on who is to have the loot."

His final conclusion was that the profit belonged to the public, and he arrived at it by this process of thought:

"Take the wage side. Wages furnish purchasing power, and the whole of business depends on people who are able to buy and pay. On the other hand, when special pleaders begin to declare that wages should absorb all the economies, all the increased profit made possible by industrial improvements, it becomes necessary to call attention to the class nature of that limited point of view. Most of our improvements are internal, that is, they occur within the management of the business, the laying out of the work, the simplifying of the method, the saving of useless labor and wasted material, all of which permits the service to be rendered at less cost than formerly.

"There are three ways in which this decreased cost, which is really increased profit, might go. We could say: We will keep it all, because it was our ability that made it possible. Or we could say: We will put it into the wage envelopes. Or we could say: It costs less to produce this thing, therefore the selling price ought to be reduced to give the buyer the benefit.

"In the first instance the argument would be: The extra profit belongs to those whose brains made it possible. In the second instance the argument would be: The extra profit belongs to the workers, they are the producers. In the third instance the argument would be: The buying public has the right to necessities and service at the lowest possible cost.

"Stating the arguments gives the answer. The benefit belongs to the public. The owners and the workers will get their reward by the increased amount of business the lower prices bring. Industry cannot exist for a class." *

The only source of profit was work—not hard work

* *Today and Tomorrow,* by Henry Ford. Copyright 1926 by Doubleday & Co., Inc.

but work well done. There was a difference. A man might work very hard with his hands and never make a good living. Indeed, it was self-evident that a great majority of people were not capable either mentally or physically of making a good living for themselves—that was to say, they were unable with their hands to create the amount of goods the world needed, and therefore certainly not enough to exchange for the goods they themselves needed. That was where the machine came in.

His definition of work well done was to create something that satisfied a human want and sell it at a price everybody could afford to pay. That meant to create it in great quantity. Men working with their hands could never produce that result, nor could they ever earn high wages. Moreover, you would never be able to find enough men with skill in their hands. "A million men working with their hands," he said, "could never approximate our daily output." And even if they could, how could you manage a million men? But if you built skill into the machine, set the machines close together, and caused the material to flow continuously through them, then you did two things at once, namely, you made it possible for even unskilled workers to earn high wages and, secondly, with the product you satisfied human wants that could not otherwise have been satisfied at all—provided only the workers were willing to mind the machines with diligence.

That was the pattern. Ford went so much further

22

and faster with it than anybody else that it came to be known as the Ford idea.

Some said he had taken skill out of work. His answer was that by putting higher skill into planning, management and tool building, he made it possible for skill to be enjoyed by the man who was not skilled.

4

THE material effects were astounding. It was a method that did multiply wealth in a marvelous manner. It made it possible for anybody to own an automobile, including every Ford worker.

But it had other effects concerning which there could be diverse opinions. It required of the worker a kind of automatism corresponding to that of the machine he minded. He could not stop, nor slow down, because it was all in one moving chain.

The norm of efficiency—even that was transferred from the individual to the group. The individual in his own free way might be able to produce more than the average, but as one of a group there would be no point in it, for then he would have to wait on the others; on the other hand, if he produced less than the average he slowed down the work and was removed.

But man is not an efficient animal really. He likes to pause, to look at the chips, smoke, walk about a little, and then return to his work by an impulse and rhythm of his own. Secondly, it required a regimentation of the

23

workers all the way down to the movements of their feet while at work.

For example, the piston rod assembly. It was a very simple operation. The foreman could not understand why it should take three minutes. He analyzed the motions with a stop watch. Four hours out of a day were spent in walking, as the assembler gathered in his materials and pushed away his finished work. The operation was split into three parts, a slide was put on the bench, three men on each side of it and an inspector at the end. One man then performed only one third of the operation without shifting his feet. Where twenty-eight men had turned out 175 assemblies a day, now seven men turned out 2,600.

Some of the repetitive work was so monotonous that Ford himself wondered how a man could stick to it. There was one man who did nothing but dredge small gears in a vat of oil at the end of a rod and drop them one at a time in a basket. This required neither intelligence nor energy, yet he did that and nothing else for eight years, saved his wages and resisted any attempt to move him to another job, confirming Ford in the opinion that "the average worker wants a job in which he does not have to think."

And perhaps it would be just as well for a man not to think; the machine could do his thinking for him. There was one who got to thinking he was lopsided, but that turned out to be something that had happened not to his body but to his mind. Ford told the story to

24

prove his case that repetitive labor was not harmful: "There was one case of a man who all day long did little but step on a treadle release. He thought the motion was making him one-sided. The medical examination did not show that he had been affected. But of course he was changed to a job that used another set of muscles. In a few weeks he asked for his old job back."

To save time and overhead and to keep the feet still, machines were placed closer and closer together until you might have thought they were jammed; but the room a machine worker needed had been calculated to the inch; also the cubic content of the air space above him, so that each one got the necessary amount of oxygen, and none wasted. "We put more machinery per square foot of floor space than any other factory in the world," said Ford. "Every foot of space not used carries an overhead expense. No man has too much room and no man has too little."

By the mechanical extension of the man the productive power of labor was enormously increased. Thus an hour of labor, being more productive, could be more highly rewarded. If you were going to keep wages going up and prices going down, as Ford intended, there was no other way to do it, and so far all to the good. But man is more than a vessel of labor. This was something that had happened to him. His role in it was passive. And thoughtful people began now to ask seriously for the first time:

Which is the slave—man or machine?

25

Ford's answer was to pose the problem of a man unable to earn a good living without machinery. Would you withhold the machinery because attendance upon it may be monotonous? Or would you put him in the way of a good living? And would a man be happier for using the machine to less than its capacity? Would he be happier for producing less than he might and consequently getting less than his share of the world's goods in exchange?

The less the machine requires of the worker in the way of skill the more it demands of him in the way of obedience, and this to the point at which you may hardly say which is acting—the reflex of the machine or the reflex of the worker who releases its power by stepping on a treadle or touching a button. In the hands of a skilled mechanic the hammer and chisel are obedient to his will, and it is a beautiful thing to watch. Set a dozen cutting tools in an automatic machine, driven by power, so that to produce a certain predetermined transformation of the raw material the worker has only to perform a series of perfunctory motions, and what have you? The man who performs the perfunctory motions must absolutely obey the principles of the machine. Put thousands of such machines side by side with a perfunctory man in front of each one, then see that the material flows, and you have mass production. But you have also the necessity for extreme discipline. The man must be an automaton too.

This Ford would not deny. Men had to do as they were told. No organization so highly specialized, one part so dependent on another, could permit human beings to be willful. Without the most rigid discipline there would be hopeless confusion. He thought it could not and should not be otherwise in industry.

The man will work fewer hours. He will exert himself less to produce more. He will have more time for play afterward, and the money to play with; but the hand at work will have no time for gladness.

He did not believe in the glad hand. He did not believe in the personal touch. It was too late for that. A great business was really too big to be human. It had supplanted the personality of the man. There were men who must always have an atmosphere of good feeling around them before they could do their work. In the end they were failures. There was too much reliance on good feeling in business organizations generally. He wanted as little as possible of the personal element. It was not necessary for people to love each other in order to work together. Too much good-fellowship could be a very bad thing, with one man trying to cover up the faults of another. Some organizations used up so much energy and time maintaining a feeling of harmony that they had no force left to work for the object for which the organization was created. A factory was not a drawing room. There need not be much personal contact. Simply, a man did his work and went home.

5

THESE are hard sayings. To do his work with no gladness in it and then go home. Was that what a mass production worker was for?

Henry Ford's answer to that question was both yes and no. The *yes* meant that the worker was an eight-hour automaton, serving the strict demands of the industrial process. In that character he was a Ford invention. The *no* meant that for the rest of his time the man was a human being with a free life to live. Even as an automaton he was better off than he had ever been before, for if he were not here performing repetitive tasks in this clean and air-conditioned environment he would be selling his muscle in animal drudgery, digging ditches in the sun or trying to wangle a living out of a Kentucky hill farm.

If the appearances were that the machine enslaved him, even for eight hours, you were obliged to consider what the machine had done for him in his other character as a free human being. It enabled him to go home earlier, to have a house such as no other unskilled worker had ever been able to afford, and to go to and fro in an automobile of his own. Beyond all that, you had to think of him impersonally, in relation to a machine organization which, for all its hardness, did multiply the wealth and leisure of society and increase the satisfaction of everyday living in a fabulous manner.

It would have been easier for the mass production worker to see himself as Ford saw him but for a certain contradiction. He was expected at the same time to be a self-resourceful individual in all circumstances, so that if he offended the deity and got fired or if the machine stopped, as it sometimes did, he could go forth on his own and take care of himself.

An idle machine creates no wealth, but neither does it eat. An idle man likewise creates no wealth, and yet he must eat. Here an impasse occurs between two ways of thinking.

In Henry Ford's philosophy, the machine was an elemental force, blindly creative, like nature. How to release it was man's greatest discovery. The consequences were social and tremendous and might bring many new problems, but these would be problems of hitherto unimagined plenty, and you might trust them to solve themselves; or you might think of the consequences as you think of food as a consequence of rain. But if the machine were not held relentlessly to its elemental function the magnificent effects either would not follow or would be in any case less extravagant. Therefore the machine must not be worried about the individual, any more than nature is. Consider nature, how thoughtful she is for the species and how careless of the single member.

Ford once said that industry does not exist to support people.

That was the kind of startling thought that often grew on the Ford tree, like an air plant, with apparently no roots at all.

If industry does not exist to support people, what is it for?

His answer was that the purpose of industry was to multiply and cheapen the cost of things that satisfy human wants.

To do its job properly it had to be efficient; to be efficient it had to be impersonal and ruthless, according to the laws of its own necessities. You could build skill into the machine; you could not build into it both skill and sentiment. Social ideas such as continuity of employment or spreading the work were sentimental.

It might well be that some parts of industry were better off working on a seasonal basis. In that case seasonal unemployment was not the industry's fault but the fault of men looking for a year's support from an industry that could give only half a year's work. If an industry could work steadily through the whole year, so much the better, but continuous employment must not be gained by spreading work and wages thin. Nothing was to be gained by thinking in that direction.

Yet he himself had been sometimes obliged to act in that direction. He had been forced in some emergencies to depart from this policy, spreading work among a number of men, giving each man a few days a week. But he regarded it as a makeshift and, in this scientific age, one that industry ought to be ashamed of.

30

Whatever went wrong with his theory, this one or any other, the fault was with people. If all industry were scientifically organized and efficiently managed, then human livelihood, he thought, could be made as secure as the supply lines that brought raw material to the machines, and the basis of a home could be as solid as the basis of a factory; and if, for all that, it should happen that a man found himself out of a job, he could very easily save himself. How? That also was simple.

The trouble with a man out of a job was that he went looking for another job instead of looking for work. If he looked for work he was bound to find it. Ford said of himself that he had often been out of a job but never out of work.

There was always plenty of work for everyone; it was not possible for any man to do useful work without in some fashion receiving adequate payment. He thought that if the jobless men even in the big cities would attack the work they might see everywhere waiting to be done, they would quickly find that they had made good jobs for themselves, instead of waiting for jobs. Let them seek work before wages.

Such was the philosophy with which Henry Ford approached the tragic failure of his career. This is remembered as a failure in labor relationship. Its meaning was much more than that. It was the failure to create a satisfactory race of machine people; or perhaps it was only that he tried to create it before its time.

31

6

HIS feelings for people were those of a shy, sensitive, egotistical man; but his feeling for the machine was an original passion. One may believe that he was the first to see what the machine was for. The right use of it was not simply to increase the leverage of man's animal power, so that he might perform his work with less exertion. No. But if you learned its inexorable laws and obeyed them the machine would transform society in a wonderful manner, set it free from immemorial and wasteful drudgeries, fill its life with new and miraculous things, and give it time to enjoy them.

A world that never could be made with hands.

If you regard the machine in that light you may see that its demands will be imperious. Once it was that a man could think of the machine as serving him. Then a time of paradox comes. The machine itself demands to be served, for unless it is served according to its own laws it will be unable to perform its miracle.

Does it then enslave the man who serves it?

Ford said no. The only slave left on earth was man minus the machine. That you could see in other lands—men and women hauling wood and stone and water on their backs, artisans clumsily spending long hours in toil for a paltry result, low standards of life, poverty to the edge of disaster. Such were the conditions where men had not learned the secrets of the machine.

Yet as you watched the men on the Ford assembly line there was no doubt about what you saw. The machine was not the hand of the man extended; the man was the hand of the machine. The man was serving the machine, and the service was both docile and servile. If the hand failed the hand was wrong and the machine was right.

If from the end of the assembly line you followed the automobile out into the world, then you saw what Ford meant. Unless human beings were serving the machine, and serving it according to its own law, people could not have these automobiles. And you might understand also what Ford meant when he said it was a sin—a sin against the welfare of society—to use a machine at less than its full capacity. "Is the man happier"—the man who serves the machine—"for producing less than he might and consequently getting less than his share of the world's goods in exchange?"

But the feeling of the normal mass production worker was compounded of neither affection nor gratitude. He did not invent the machine. It was not a tool he could select or fashion to fit his hand. It was the hand of him that had to fit the machine; he could touch the machine only by a series of disciplined dexterities, to actuate it; and if anything went wrong he could not fix it. An expert was called to do that. Certainly he could never have that feeling for the machine that a woodsman has for his ax or the old-fashioned mechanic

33

for his hammer and cold chisel, with which he could smooth a plate of steel as if it had been passed through a planing lathe.

And as for seeing how it transformed the world, even a world that included him—well, yes, he could see that dimly; and yet he knew that in that same world, for all its high common welfare, the anxieties of life were still acute and personal. That he might own an automobile made it not always easier and sometimes even harder to take home the bacon.

The world that Henry Ford imagined, with every home as solid as a factory, did not exist, any more than the contented mass production worker.

So long as the Ford wage was incomparably the highest wage for unskilled and semiskilled men, the Ford worker was loyal to the Ford job, but even this was more fear of losing the job than loyalty. During this time Ford evidently thought he was creating a race of docile machine people. They willingly stretched themselves and submitted to the machine's discipline, which was terrific.

But when the prevailing industrial wage in the Detroit region began to catch up with the Ford wage, so that workers could choose, the loyalty of the Ford worker was much short of what Ford expected. When the wage at General Motors or at Chrysler or any other automobile plant was as high as the Ford wage, the picture began to change. Ford's "wage motive theory" of industry could not perform repetitive miracles; and

34

his advantage as the manufacturer who paid the highest wage and had therefore the lowest labor cost was lost.

Partly it was transferred to the motor industry as a whole. As a high-wage industry, owing principally to Ford's example, it was for a long time practically a union-free industry. Unionism was defeated by the high wage. What had unionism to offer to these workers?

7

THEN came the Great Depression, and with it the Wagner Labor Act, which transferred power from management to labor; and the unions moved in, led by John L. Lewis. The wage rate was still high, but the wage rate was no longer the measure of labor's welfare. What mattered was the take-home pay, that is to say, the bacon; and what with the distress of unemployment and the hardships of part time at the high wage rate, labor in the Detroit region was in great trouble.

The union leadership was adroit. First, General Motors was struck, and while its plants were down Ford and Chrysler went on making cars. General Motors could not stand that for long.

During a celebrated conference in the governor's office at Lansing, Walter Chrysler beat his fist on the table and said to Lewis:

"This isn't fair. You shut us down one at a time."

Lewis said:

"Chrysler, that's the first reasonable thing you've said since this conference started. I agree with you. It isn't fair. And I'll tell you how we'll fix it. Tomorrow I'll close you all down."

After that Chrysler threw in the sponge and signed a labor contract.

That left Ford, alone of the Big Three, standing by himself. For a long time he stood alone against the union.

Because he was going to be a very tough customer the union hesitated to take him head on, preferring rather to build up a legal case against him before the National Labor Relations Board. The Ford Motor Company's violations of the law were flagrant and contemptuous. The behavior of its workers was the concern of the largest and perhaps the most ruthless private police force that was ever known in American industry. Every worker suspected the man at his side, who might be a company informer; if he went to a union meeting he was watched; if he indicated a sympathy for unions he was fired.

I said to Ford at this time: "You are going to lose this fight."

He asked: "Why do you say that?"

I said: "Because you are on the wrong side of the law."

His answer was: "There is a law of the job higher than any law Congress can pass. The law of the job will prevail."

His feeling against unions was bitter and personal. It rested on two grounds. First, he intensely resented

36

the idea that unions could do more for Ford workers than he did for them. Secondly, unions committed the unforgivable sin of interfering with the machine. They slowed it down. They insisted on running it at less than its full capacity. That was to say, as was already evident in the General Motors and Chrysler contracts, they laid their hands on production. They bargained about how fast the assembly line should run.

The feud was desperate and ugly on both sides. There were scenes of violence at the gates.

But the tide of a new social order was irresistibly rising. Labor was arriving. No single large organization of industry, not even the Ford Motor Company, could afford not to make peace with it. The law was on the side of labor, and under the law the union had built a case so damaging that a complete public revelation of it might have destroyed the myth that the Ford worker was the contented darling of mass production, who never would have wavered in his loyalty but for the nefarious activities of the union leaders, egged on perhaps by rival industrialists and Wall Street. The most ardent believer in this myth to the very end was Ford himself. He never understood why he had failed.

When at last he surrendered he did a characteristic thing. He went overboard. He gave the union more than it asked for. He signed a contract more favorable to labor than General Motors or Chrysler or any other competitor had signed—a contract that provided for compulsory unionism in Ford plants, the collection of

37

union dues by the management out of the pay envelope, a union label for Ford products and badges for all members of the plant police, so that never again would they be able to infiltrate themselves among the workers.

Was it a victory over Ford, as labor thought, or was it a victory over the machine?

In either case, as you may suppose, it was too much for the hotheads. Where before workers were not permitted to smoke anywhere on the premises or to lounge at ease when the assembly line broke down, now they dragged in vats of victory beer, played craps in their leisure moments, smoked as they liked, and made anybody's tiff with a foreman the occasion for a wildcat strike.

At last the union leaders had the good sense to side with management in forbidding wildcat strikes, on pain of lay-off or discharge. The machine commanded order. That was its minimum exaction.

Later Ford was induced to meet the labor leader who had beaten him. William C. Richards, in *The Last Billionaire*,* relates that Ford said to the labor leader: "It was a sensible thing we did, getting you into the plant."

The labor leader said: "That's what we think. We didn't know you thought so."

Ford said: "Well, you've been fighting General Motors and the Wall Street crowd. Now you are in here and we have given you a union shop and more than you

* *The Last Billionaire,* by William C. Richards. Charles Scribner's Sons, 1948.

got out of them. That puts you on our side, doesn't it?
We fight them together from now on, don't we?"

A brave and rueful statement, tainted by a lifelong
superstition concerning his imaginary enemies and mel-
ancholy in the twilight of his career.

More and more after that it was the organization
that carried on. The tyrant's hand relaxed. His most
dogmatic theory had been badly damaged. Was it un-
sound? In any case, it assumed a world that did not
exist. Perhaps it was only misplaced in time.

8

B u t in the Ford cosmos there was an astronomical
first law that never failed. You could not define it, or if
you could it would be something else. It came to be a
disembodied force in itself, like a demon spirit, demanding sacrifice, burnt offerings and worshipful rites. Its
name was production.

The spectacle of production is visible phenomena,
and yet incomprehensible to the mind. There is no point
of view from which you can see where it begins or how,
or what moves it. In a moment of bemusement the
thought may occur to you that what you are looking
at is planetary. It moves itself. Nobody does it. Human
agencies are present and accessory, but somehow ir-
relevant, as if it were necessary only that people should
have something to do.

I knew a Ford production boss who once dreamed it
that way. He saw the mighty plant as a whole, produc-

tion taking place at high speed as if the feud with time might be lost, finished automobiles chopping off like sausages at the end of the assembly line at the rate of one a minute, and not one human being there, union or nonunion—only Ford as a phantom in every doorway, holding a stop watch. And coming awake from the dream was not like a return from anywhere strange, because it had seemed so almost real.

The struggle with union labor came to a crisis in wartime. A conflict of such bitterness might have been expected to wreck production. It did not. The Ford contribution to national defense was, nevertheless, prodigious—a contribution of things the great mechanics had never made before, such as guns and gun mounts, tanks, amphibious vehicles, aircraft engines and bomber parts; and the Willow Run bomber plant, designed by Sorensen, to cut off a bomber an hour at the end of the assembly line, was epic.

9

IT WOULD never have occurred to Ford to think labor had been ungrateful. It was only that the mind of unionism had not been able to understand what he called the wage motive for industry, over the profit motive. His theory of the wage motive forbade him to expect gratitude. When he doubled wages in the first demonstration, and when after that he raised them again, generosity was ruled out. It had to pay. It had to benefit everybody—the consumer, the wage earner and the

Ford Motor Company. When organized labor rejected his wage motive theory, in fact ruined it, the old disastrous fallacy was restored—the fallacy, namely, that the rate of wage was determined by the bargaining power of labor acting against the monopoly power of the employer.

High wages, he insisted, were more important to business than to labor. Low wages would break industry much more quickly than they would break labor.

He was thinking there not of old industry but of new industry, based on mass production. And why would low wages break that kind of industry sooner than labor? Because an underpaid man was a customer reduced in buying power. He was a poor customer. If you reduced wages you actually reduced work because you reduced the demand for work.

There was in fact no standard of wages, no limitation upon them except that set by the efficiency of industry pursuing the wage motive. If you set yourself to pay high wages, then you would find methods of manufacturing that would make high wages cheap wages.

Nor was the wage motive theory in any sense a social theory. Nearly every social theory, he believed, was a formula for living without work. And the world being what it was, all such theories could lead only to poverty because they were not productive.

Nevertheless, the impact of the original five-dollar day upon the lives of Ford workers was so terrific that he felt he had to look at what they did with the money.

Did they use it to improve their standard of living or did they waste it? So he was persuaded to set up a Social Department, with a staff of trained social service workers, to impose upon these high wage people a code of living. They had to be sober, they had to like work and they had to be family-loving. Since now for the first time they could afford decent homes, they were forbidden to take in boarders. That was a custom among them that made the home "a place to make money out of rather than a place to live in."

That was his first experience with paternalism. In a few years he was sick of it. He distrusted social service workers as a strange race and their language bothered him. Suddenly, out went the Social Department. Let people manage their own lives.

What if they did not use their spare time to the best advantage? That was not for the Ford Motor Company to say, provided their work was better. The average man would find his own best way, even though that way might not exactly fit into the programs of the social reformers.

Although the fact that people had more leisure and more money was wonderful in itself, it was nothing they should be expected to feel grateful for. The truth was that to provide more leisure, and then the money with which people could enjoy it, had become a *necessity* of mass production industry.

Why? Well, was not the influence of the shorter work week on consumption obvious? If factories generally

42

went back to the ten-hour day, industry would suffer because people would not have time to consume the goods produced. For instance, a workman would have little use for an automobile if he had to be in the shop from dawn to dark. Of course there was a humanitarian side to the shorter day and the shorter week, but dwelling on that side was likely to distort the view, for then leisure might be put before work, instead of after work, where it belonged.

And that was something the machine had done. That was the world that could not have been made by hands. The hours of work, he insisted, were regulated by the machine and by the large-scale organization of work and by nothing else.

That was in 1930. He could see no limit to it.

Paternalism, moreover, had an air of charity about it, and that he hated; he thought very ill of charity. "It is a drug," he said. There were emergencies when men and women, and especially children, needed help, but these cases were not actually as numerous as they seemed to be. The very fact that charity could be had increased them, for charity held out the promise of something for nothing. The cases of real need could be looked after on a personal basis without destroying, as by the machinery of organized charity, the values of self-respect.

All of his own charities were governed by that theme. He once made a home for orphans and afterward told of his disappointment with it. Once a week he went to see how it was getting on. The managers, who were supposed to be qualified men, seemed to think of it as a place in which to confine children. So he scrapped it and got the children adopted into private homes. The sickliest boy of all was adopted by a woman who already had six of her own.

From all of these excursions he came back to the same place. What mattered above all was the wage. Not a social wage, not a generous wage, not a wage arrived at by the bargaining power of either labor or the employer, but a scientific wage determined by the wage motive. There was no social service that could take the place of wages. Let the wage be the highest that mass production could afford to pay and you would not have to worry much about people. It was very simple, really. Any confusion about it could usually be traced back "to an unwillingness on the part of someone to work." It was management's part so to arrange and organize work that it could produce high wages, but the starting point of high wages was the willingness to work. Without that willingness, management was powerless.

And that held as much for work of the mind as for work of the hand.

How long could industry last on the purchasing power of those whose income was independent of what they received from work? The country was maintained by work. And the evidence of work was wages.

SEEDS OF THE MONKEY WRENCH

For the grand mechanics work was play. If it had not been play it would have killed them. They were as men possessed. They often forgot to eat. As they drove the workers, so they drove themselves, only much harder; and machines they drove until the metal ached.

Once some machine builders were called in to bid on a special machine. The specifications called for a speed that would produce two hundred finished parts an hour. The machine builders said: "You have made a mistake here. You meant to say two hundred a day." The Ford engineer who had made the design was called in. He said: "There is no mistake. Two hundred an hour." The machine builders said: "No machine can do that." The engineer said: "Before asking you to make it we made one for ourselves, to see if it would work. It's working now. Come and see it."

For a new machine that worked or a new wrinkle that gave time another kick in the pants their glee was like that of children with a wonderful toy. If the idea had come from a foreman, or a worker, as sometimes happened, Ford would stuff the man's pocket with money on the spot. Yet no sooner had it worked than they all began to think of ways to make it work better, and if anybody could think of a way to do that the wonderful toy was broken up for scrap.

When it was the wonder plant of the world for doing impossible things in unheard-of ways they were still so sure they could do every thing still better that anybody was welcome to come and look, even rival motorcar makers, Ford saying: "If they can do it better than we do it they are welcome to it. Then we will go and look at what they do."

What moved them? You may think of several motivations.

There is pride in belonging to the most famous crew in the world, even though your own part in it may be small. If you are on the top side of a crew like that you have of course a sense of achievement by association. Moreover, since it was a monarchy, almost anyone might hope to be struck by the Cinderella lightning. When a man was called from his work to go immediately to the office it could be either that he was important enough to get fired by a high executive or that he was about to be invested with a fragment of the magic carpet, holding in his hand the Ford wand that commanded men and materials in a very imperious manner. He might be sent to open a coal mine, to run a railroad or to revolution-

46

ize a lumber operation, and if he knew nothing about mining or railroading or lumbering, that was all the better. Whatever the task might be, it was supposed that he could do it better than anyone had done it before if only he possessed these four qualifications, namely, common sense, drive, a direct way of seeing and the Ford credo, which was: "We do it our way." His instructions were always simple. Go do it. If he couldn't, another would.

All of this could happen because Ford did not believe in experts. "Our men are not experts," he said. "We have most unfortunately found it necessary to get rid of a man as soon as he thinks himself an expert. The moment one gets into the expert state of mind a great number of things become impossible. Our new operations are always directed by men who have no previous knowledge of the subject and therefore have not had a chance to get on really familiar terms with the impossible."

One of his illustrations was glass. He thought plate glass could be made continuously in a big ribbon with no hand work at all. The glass experts of the world said all of that had been thought of before and tried and it could not be done. He gave the task of doing it to men who had never been in a glass plant.

They did it with such marvelous success that now everybody makes plate glass that way.

If experts were needed, they could always be hired, but no Ford operation was ever directed by a technician. He always knew too many things that couldn't be done, whereas a Ford man could do anything because he didn't know any better. The Ford man's role was to say to the expert: "Do it anyhow."

The question was: What moved them? The answers that have been given are all reasonable and valid, with only this reservation, that it was not a famous crew in the beginning and there was not always a Ford wand. That also had to be created.

Do you say, perhaps, it was profit, or the hope of profit? This calls for a discussion that belongs in another place, by itself. It is true that Ford was the greatest profit maker of his time. It is true also that alone among the industrialists of his time or any other time he sincerely challenged the profit motive. More of this later. It is the enigma that lies at the very core of the story of a world that almost was.

No. What moved them was something that was there from the start.

2

E v e n so, the beginning took place under appearances which were in every way ordinary, with no signs or omens whatever. If you had witnessed it you would not remember it as anything uncommon. The same thing was happening at the same time in other places.

In a low frame building, 25 by 250 feet, you might have seen some perspiring men putting together what still were called horseless carriages. They had no machinery—only tools like monkey wrenches, hammers,

48

screw drivers and pliers—because machinery was costly and they could not afford to buy it. The horseless carriage was not made here. The engines were made by a distant machine shop at so much apiece, the bodies were made by a carriage company, the wheels by a wheel company, and so on; and all that these men were doing was to assemble a horseless carriage from finished parts delivered at the door by horse-drawn drays. They expected to assemble ten a day. They expected also, as they sold the ten a day, to be able to pay the machine shop for the engines, the carriage shop for the bodies, the wheel company for the wheels, et cetera, and they had to do it fast with no mishap, for they had almost no money at all.

The boss mechanic, who was also vice-president and general manager, might have been seen helping to nail the completed jobs into a boxcar for shipment, with mail piling up on a little upstairs desk for a month, because nobody could take the time to open it. When at last they hired a bookkeeper, he found two wastebaskets full of unopened letters, some of them containing checks.

You would not have remembered the boss mechanic. He was a thin, tall, deep-eyed man, alternately impish and austere, who couldn't be still. He had designed the engine that came from the machine shop. His name was on the horseless carriage.

Ten years before with his own hands he had made an automobile buggy; it was neither the first nor the best

49

one. He had built a racing car—the famous 999—that uttered flames from the exhaust and sounded like the jungle in an animal panic; but others too had built racing cars and his was only a little bit faster. He was one of a number of men celebrated in automobile history who for years had been blowing themselves up in their woodsheds and kitchens trying to find out what happened when a mixture of air and gasoline was ignited in a cylinder—and they were all nuts. As a pioneer manufacturer of motorcars he had already failed twice, losing his backers' money, and that was about the average.

It was a time when adventuresome men with a little money and a dim prevision of the motorcar industry were looking for inventors on whom to make their bets; and it often happened that they made their bets secretly, fearful that if their conservative business associates, and especially their bankers, found out what they were doing they would be written off as loony visionaries.

Several of these, having looked over the field, picked on Henry Ford, partly on their guess that he was a good inventor and partly because he had a name that might help to sell a car—the name of a man who had built the fastest racing car and had driven it himself. In *My Life and Work* he remembered his last race, the purpose of which was to advertise the Ford car, already on the market. This was his recollection of it:

"Winning a race or making a record was then the

best kind of advertising. So I fixed up the Arrow, the twin of the old 999—in fact practically remade it—and a week before the New York automobile show I drove it myself over a surveyed mile straightaway on the ice. I shall never forget that race. The ice seemed smooth enough, so smooth that if I had called off the trial we should have secured an immense amount of the wrong kind of advertising; but instead of being smooth, that ice was seamed with fissures which I knew were going to mean trouble the moment I got up speed. But there was nothing to do but go through with the trial, and I let the old Arrow out. At every fissure the car leaped into the air. I never knew how it was coming down. When I wasn't in the air I was skidding; but somehow I stayed top side up and on the course, making a record that went all over the world." *

His biographers note that he celebrated his survival, and the record, with a muskrat dinner cooked on the spot and eaten with the man who rode along to cut off the fuel by hand in case the control mechanism froze.

3

THE men who made their bets on Ford were a coal dealer, the coal dealer's bookkeeper and his sister, a banker who trusted the coal dealer, two brothers who owned the machine shop that made the engines, a car-

* *My Life and Work,* by Henry Ford. Copyright 1922 by Doubleday & Co., Inc.

penter, two lawyers, a clerk, the owner of a notions store and a man who made windmills and air rifles. The engine builders put in their good will. The carpenter put in a frame building. The total amount of cash raised among them was twenty-eight thousand dollars.

One of the lawyers, who was going to put in five thousand dollars, accounted for it in a letter to his father, saying:

"Through the country Mr. Ford is looked upon as an expert. He has won numerous racing contests and is widely known, which will be a big asset in his own car sales. The old machine which he built he sold to his former backers when he retired. He did reserve the right of his own name. They cannot take that away from him. . . . The parts are to be made under contract. . . . A small assembling plant will be rented to the company at $75 a month. In this plant there will be ten or twelve men at $1.50 a day, together with a fore-man. You can see how small the manufacturing expense will be. . . . It looks like a certain fifty per cent profit. . . . They are to deliver ten machines a day. . . . It is amazing the way the thing has been started. Everything has been done since last October. Other companies with half a dozen draftsmen under lock and key have been three years making the same progress."

That was in 1903.

Ten years later every other car you saw on the road was a Ford. The sounds of the Model T—its gutturals and verbs and lamentations and chortling—were the

52

overtones of the American way of life. At Highland Park, in a suburban area of Detroit, was the largest automobile factory in the world, turning out a complete car every three minutes—and the boss mechanic was the same man still.

By this time he had bought out all the other stockholders, so that never again when they thought he was mad could they threaten to take him to court. They had thought he was mad when he said he was going to make automobiles at the rate of one a minute. Then in a little while, from the sour grape arbor, they saw him do it.

But even yet he had not arrived. He was on his way.

After Highland Park, where at length Model T's did depart under their own power from the end of the assembly line at the rate of one a minute—after that came the mighty River Rouge plant at Dearborn.

That was the beginning of empire. It seemed to rise as if it contained a principle of self-creation. Ford said, "Put it here," and there it was. So Alexander made cities to appear.

It had a river God made, not a very efficient river, and Ford dug the harbor that God forgot in order to receive ships from the inland sea. Besides ships of its own, it had its own coal and iron and lead mines, its own railroad, its own forests and sawmills. It had organs and operations in every important American city and in Canada, Europe, South America and Asia.

Anything it needed it could make for itself, and many things it made just to learn how in case its suppliers

53

should begin to charge too much, or as insurance against the failure of its outside sources of supply. It made steel, machines, tools, the finest precision gauges in the world, glass, artificial leather, textiles, paper, cement, electric locomotives, chemicals, hydroelectric dams and airplanes. It built its own power plants, its own steam turbines and generators.

After World War I it bought a lot of Liberty Ships for scrap and then built a pair of shears to slice them up as if they were cheese.

For grand mechanics, this was Heaven. Anything they saw or anything they imagined, that they could do. The government wanted some antisubmarine boats, provided they could be built in a great hurry without interfering with any other war work. In 120 days, at River Rouge, there was a building a quarter of a mile long, 350 feet wide and 100 feet high, and inside of it Eagle Boats, stamped out of sheet steel like automobile bodies, were being engined and equipped—and this the work not of marine engineers but of mechanics who had never built a boat before.

At a nod from the boss mechanic prodigious feats were lightly undertaken and performed with the air of conjury. To uproot the entire tractor plant from the bank of the River Rouge and set it down in Ireland was a mere chore.

And this behemoth by exerting itself could produce in the world automobiles at the rate of one every ten seconds.

54

If you say, "And all of that in one working lifetime from an original cash capital of twenty-eight thousand dollars," the answer is yes, as a matter of fact. That was all the money that anybody ever put in. From that time on the business made its own capital. But that is only to say—what? That one acorn grew in a fabulous manner. Why did this one grow so big and tall? Was it a true fact of nature or a capricious event out of order?

That is what now stands to be explored.

THREE

GENESIS AND EVOLUTION

THE jigsaw itself was a little crazy. You may identify the interlocking pieces. They are five, and you may name them as the *car*, the *time*, the *idea*, the *method* and the *man*; but when you have fitted them together you find something like a key piece missing. This you may call the *X* piece. It will turn out to be not a fact but a truth, touching the acorn.

So first the car.

During the first five years the Ford Motor Company made eight different models, some with two cylinders, some with four and one with six; some with a chain drive and some with a shaft drive, and one with the engine behind the driver's seat. They were all good cars, as cars were then, and relatively cheap; and they sold so well that the business flourished. The original factory space had expanded five-fold in Detroit, there were fourteen branch houses, and the output was one hundred cars a day, when several of the eleven other stockholders became uneasy. They thought that was success enough. In *My Life and Work* Ford wrote:

"They wanted to do something to stop me from ruining the company, and when I replied to the effect that one hundred cars a day was only a trifle and that I hoped before long to make a thousand a day, they were inexpressibly shocked and, as I understand, seriously contemplated court action. If I had followed the general opinion of my associates I should have kept the business about as it was, put our funds into a fine administration building, tried to make bargains with such competitors as seemed too active, made new designs from time to time to catch the fancy of the public, and generally have passed into the position of a quiet respectable citizen with a quiet respectable business." *

There were omens now, but they were still so dim that even the few who thought they could see them had moments of doubt and panic. They might have been hypnotized by a man who kept thinking out loud about a universal car for the people at the price of a horse and buggy.

He was by this time in control of the company, having a clear majority of the stock in his name, and could do as he pleased, unless his associates took him to court to protect their profits from his devouring imagination. They actually did that later.

One morning in 1909, with no warning to anybody, he announced that he was going to make only one car—and it would be the Model T. One might have it as a

---

* *My Life and Work,* by Henry Ford. Copyright 1922 by Doubleday & Co., Inc.

roadster or as a coupé, which was a difference of body only, and the buyer could have it any color he liked provided he wanted it black. In every other way these Model T's would be all exactly alike. His public announcement read:

"I will build a motor car for the great multitude. It will be large enough for the family but small enough for the individual to run and care for. It will be constructed of the best materials, by the best men to be hired, after the simplest designs that modern engineering can devise. But it will be so low in price that no man making a good salary will be unable to own one—and enjoy with his family the blessing of hours of pleasure in God's great open spaces."

In the next nineteen years he made fifteen million of them.

As Ford saw it the Model T had but four essentials. They were the power plant, the frame, the front axle and the rear axle, all so designed that no special skill would be required to repair or replace them. Any member of the male race could take it apart and put it together again.

Ford's intention was to make the parts first interchangeable and then so simple and inexpensive that the owner of a car would never hire a mechanic. The parts would cost so little that it would be cheaper to buy new ones than to have old ones repaired, and they could be carried in hardware shops like nails or bolts.

Those who can remember their Model T days will be

reminded of how they used to take the car apart with a monkey wrench and pliers, put the used or damaged parts in a gunny sack, take the sack to the nearest Ford station where it would be filled with new parts in exchange for the old—and a slight difference to pay—then home to put it all together again, with a perfectly absurd sense of ego satisfaction. More Model T's were rebuilt in that manner, in barns and sheds and under the shade tree, than were ever sent to service stations.

2

IT IS impossible for members of this generation to know what a displacement the Model T had in the lives of their fathers. It was a mechanical animal such as never existed before and will never be seen again. It changed the folkways of a nation. It enriched the fund of native humor and became the butt of so many jokes that it was always on the defensive, which alone would have endeared it to a large segment of human nature. It had some of the characteristics of a mule, the patience of a camel, the courage of a bull terrier, and in bad situations it could be very gallant, although there was latent in it a whimsical hostility to the human race. When you cranked it on a cold morning it might come at you. To know if it had oil in the crankcase you had to crawl under it and fiddle with two pet cocks. To know where the gas was you had to lift the seat cushion, unscrew the cap and poke a stick into the gas tank. In emergencies it could do without either oil or gas. It had no speedometer. If you drove too fast and the engine got red hot you stopped to let it cool off. In the hills at night you could hear it, almost as one of the sounds of nature, taking a grade and saying:

Afraid-I-can't—afraid—I—can't——a-f-r-a-i-d——I——c—a—n—t——a——f——r——a——i——

Then:

YesIcanyesIcanyesIcan

That was when it was pushed into low gear and went over the top.

And it was ugly—ugly at first and uglier with the years. In the beginning it had some brass mountings and turned wooden knobs on the quadrant. These refinements disappeared one by one, until at last there was nowhere on it or in it one extra flourish of craftsmanship. This ruthless simplification took place as the price fell. "The price," said Ford, "is an integral part of the design." The price fell from $1,200 to $295, and the car became a thing of stark utility.

The loyalty of people to Model T for nearly two decades was both rational and partisan. Ford car owners were sensitive. A joke was all right if it was meant right; aspersions they resented personally. In any case, they had the unanswerable retort. The one thing it could never be accused of was failure. It never failed, or almost never, and if it did—"that," said Ford, "is my fault."

Not only was it light in weight and a high stepper for dirt roads, getting through when other cars stuck fast;

it was in all essential respects very excellently made. The choke rod might look like a piece of bailing wire, but it never broke, and the steel of the chassis, the axles and other important parts had the toughness of original sin.

Long before Model T, Ford one day picked up a stem valve from the wreck of a French racing car. It was light and very strong and nobody knew what kind of steel it was. He sent it to a metallurgist for analysis. It turned out to be vanadium steel. No American steel mill had ever made it. He brought a man from Europe who knew how and then subsidized a small steel mill to try it—"For," he said, "that is the kind of steel I want for the universal car I am going to build." After some failures he got it, and it was nearly three times as strong as the steel American motorcars until then were made of. After that he measured the demands an automobile made upon the steel in its different parts and ended by putting twenty kinds of steel in the Model T—one kind for toughness, one kind for hardness, another for elasticity, and so on.

3

AT THE age of nineteen Model T died. It froze to death.

One weakness of mass production is rigidity. Variety and quantity are strangers. If it is quantity you want you are obliged, as the engineers say, to "freeze" the design.

61

When you have miles of machines all tuned and geared in a certain way, each machine doing only the special thing it has the habit of doing, and from these machines more than one hundred thousand parts flowing with timed precision to a moving assembly line to fall exactly into place on the automobile that grows as it moves and is finished when it gets to the end of the line—then you have mass production. But obviously you cannot change the design of the automobile without tearing your factory to pieces. A change of design will mean new parts, and for new parts you will need new machines and time to teach new habits to old machines. Ford was first with this method and went further with it than anybody else, and that was why he could keep reducing the price of the car. He was continually adding new and more powerful machines, but only for the purpose of making the same car faster and faster.

So it was that year after year it was the same Model T, and the more it changed in little ways the more it was the same thing still.

Meanwhile, everything else was changing. Dirt roads turned to concrete. People grew richer and could pay more for automobiles. Other motorcar makers, following Ford's methods, were able to bring down the cost of much more attractive cars.

First the Dodge brothers, who had got very rich making Ford's engines until he began making them for himself, brought out a very good small car, and said as they did it: "Think how many Ford buyers would like to own a real automobile by paying only a little more." That was a dagger thrust.

Then General Motors began to displace Model T with its Chevrolet, as that car evolved in the hands of a production genius named William S. Knudsen, who had learned how with Ford.

Even Ford jokes had used themselves up, all but the last and most cruel one of all, from Will Rogers.

In one of its unpredictable moods the country had gone dithery over the thought of Henry Ford for President, to succeed Coolidge. Rogers drawled that to get himself elected it would be necessary for Ford to say only: "Voters, if you elect me I'll change the front end."

For a long time the boss mechanic lingered at the bedside of his creature. He could see it was very sick; he was slow to believe the disease could be fatal—the disease of change. He blamed his salesmen, the times, the mores and manners. The people were running after style; they were beguiled by appearances. The one remedy he could think of was his own patent price paregoric, but the magic was no longer in it. Fewer and fewer people wanted Model T's. That was the fact he had to face.

When at last he faced it and gave up the struggle he went overboard. He would not change the Model T. He would make a new car, from the tread up. That was the beginning of the Model A.

4

In a plant that had made 1,800,000 cars a year—
more than four a minute—everything stopped. Every
machine in it had to be remade, retaught or sent to the
furnace. Hundreds of new machines had to be invented.
An entirely new way of doing things had to be evolved.

While the Ford plant was down cold, General Motors
with its on-coming Chevrolet, and now also Chrysler
with his first car, were taking the low-priced field. Ford
dealers had nothing to sell.

Could he do it?

That became a national question. Starting from taw,
with nothing behind him but the rejected Model T,
could he produce what might be called a modern automobile good enough and soon enough to meet all this
new competition? The odds were so heavily against him,
as rational people thought, that at that time the fabulous Ford Motor Company could not have been sold in
Wall Street at five cents on the dollar.

One day the executives of a large Philadelphia advertising agency called me on the telephone. They had
taken the contract to do publicity for the new Ford car,
and one of their ideas was to take some writers out to
Dearborn to witness the evolution of it on the spot.
Would I go? I said I was intending to go out, but not
under the auspices of an advertising agency.

They said: "That's all right. Anyhow, we're not so

sure now it's a good idea. You know these people, don't you?"

I said yes, I knew them.

They said: "Let's forget the idea. Will you meet us for lunch? There's something we want to talk to you about."

At lunch they said: "Like everybody else, we've long been sold on the myth of Ford efficiency. Now we are out there looking at it. We've been there three months. We don't see it. In fact, we can hardly believe what we see."

I asked: "What do you see?"

They said: "You won't believe it either. There stands the car in the middle of the floor, nearly finished so far as we can make out. Every morning the engineers gather around it, just looking at it, waiting for Ford to appear. When he comes he reaches inside, rattles something, shakes his head and says, 'That won't do. You've got to think of something better than that.' One of them says, 'Can you think of anything, Mr. Ford?' He rattles the thing again, walks a little off and comes back, makes some pencil marks on a piece of paper, hands it to them and says, 'Try something like that.' The next morning they gather round the car again, and when Ford comes in he asks, 'Got it on?' They say, 'Yes, Mr. Ford.' He reaches in, rattles the thing again, whatever it is, makes a gesture of disgust and says, 'That's worse.' With that he walks off, leaving them

65

there gazing at the car. It's like that day after day, with the whole country screaming for the new Ford car. We don't understand it."

I said: "You don't know what you are looking at. That's invention and it cannot take place in any other way. Wait until the car is on the assembly line and then look for efficiency."

A little later I was in Dearborn. Knowing what the old practice had been, I was amazed at how they were setting up to make the new car. The crankshaft for example. Formerly, truing the forged crankshaft had been the work of a blacksmith, who held it on an anvil, sighted it, hit it here and there with a machine hammer, sighted it again, and then threw it on the pile. That was all right for the Model T. It would not do at all for the new car. Now they had a machine on which to spin the crankshaft at variable rates of speed; vibration was indicated on dials of sensitive recording instruments, and by other instruments the light and heavy spots on the forging could be exactly located for correction. That was one reason why the new car's engine was going to be much smoother than the Model T engine. And that kind of new practice went through the entire plant.

I was in Cameron's office when Ford came in. The Philadelphia advertising people were sitting in the corner, to listen. With the air of one who expects to be understood Ford said to me: "I believe in what we are doing. We had to do it. But you know, the only thing wrong with the Model T was that people got tired of looking at it."

That was, I think, the only statement of defeat I ever heard him make about anything.

I said: "The new car will be good. Everybody knows that. But the Chevrolet and the Plymouth are good cars too. What are you going to say about the new Ford car that they cannot say about theirs?"

With a gesture of impatience he replied: "I don't know. Ask the advertising people over there. That's their job."

To tease the advertising men in the corner, I said: "Do you think advertising sells a car?"

He answered shortly and emphatically: "No. A car has got to sell itself."

I asked: "Then why are you going to advertise this new car in a big way?"

At that he gave what was perhaps the best argument for advertising the listeners in the corner had ever heard, to fit a case like this.

He said: "They kept at me about it until I was sick of the subject. At last I said, 'All right. If you have to have that kind of doctor, get the best one you can find.' Since then I've been thinking about it and now I'm for it. You know why? The Ford Motor Company is so big that it has to include everything. Advertising is a special feature of the American scheme. Advertising has to live too. For that reason we have to include it."

I said: "Now you are going to make all the new cars you can and add them to the market. General Motors is going to go on making all the Chevrolets it can, and Chrysler all the Plymouths he can, whereas the total automobiles the market can absorb in a year is some definite quantity. Why can't you determine statistically what that quantity is and all govern yourselves accordingly?"

His first answer was frivolous. He said: "You want to take all the fun out of the game."

I said: "No. I'm only thinking it might be possible to bring some kind of stability into the motor industry."

"Stability," he said, as if he would bite it. "Stability is a dead fish floating downstream. The only kind of stability we know in this country is change."

"Not that," I said. "What I'm really thinking of is the recurring evil of unemployment from overproduction."

"Overproduction!" he said, more hopeful of biting that one. "It's a false word. When you say a thing has been overproduced, all you can possibly mean is that it is wrong in price or wrong in time. I suppose now you could make too many buggies at any price. They would be wrong in time."

One of his favorite maxims was that we learn as we go along. He had just learned two things. Change had killed Model T, so therefore he embraced change; and the fate of Model T was proof that a useful thing may

68

be overproduced if it is wrong in time, though it may be only that in a new time people are bored with the look of it.

This was hardly a subject that could be pursued.

I said: "Once you led everybody with service. No man with a Ford car could ever find himself far from a service station. The others have now caught up with you. They all provide excellent service, having learned it from you. What new advantage can you think of in place of that old one?"

He said: "The time is coming when an automobile will be so right that it will need no more service than a bar of soap. It will just wear out, like the one-horse shay."

5

T H E womb time of Model A was nine months. The public showing of it was a carnival event. Day after day all over the country people waited in long queues for a chance to see it. What they wanted to see much more than an automobile was whether Ford had been able to do it. He had.

It was a sane four-cylinder car, and when people said, "The Ford now is just another automobile," they meant that it had a proper gear shift and all the regular conveniences, and was no longer a species apart. The name was a guarantee of manufacturing integrity. It did more damage to the purse than the Model T, of course, and yet it was the most car for your money, and

69

the demand for it was such that one month after the first showing the Ford Motor Company was producing six thousand a day. That was 1,800,000 a year for so long as the market could stand it.

Then the same thing that had happened to Model T happened also to Model A. The design became rigid.

Meanwhile Ford's competitors continued to bring out improved models each year. From doing it and from thinking it out far ahead they had learned how to re-tool their factories for a new design and then bring it to birth with no very acute labor pains. Their annual exhibitions of more attractive cars were like fashion shows. Even if this year's car was no better than last year's, it had more frills, more eye appeal and more style. And some of the improvements were radical. General Motors offered a six-cylinder Chevrolet "for the price of a four," and Chrysler made a Plymouth with hydraulic brakes and a very sweet engine, and was so proud of it that he drove it himself to Dearborn and left it there with a taunting message for Ford. Wouldn't he like to drive a better car than his Model A? If he liked it he could keep it.

At the age of five years Model A died. It had gone out of style.

So again there had to be a new car from scratch— not a change of Model A, but something original. Again the Ford Motor Company went down cold for an indeterminate time. Again Ford dealers had nothing to sell; and this time it was so bad that they began to de-

70

sert. When they complained to Ford he said, "I don't want to know how many Chevrolet cars were sold last year nor how many will be sold this year. I don't care."

It was rumored that the new car would be an eight-cylinder job; it would be an automobile to end this silly competition once for all. A little of this news was let out to dealers, to keep them holding on, and then they heard that a terrific publicity campaign was all ready to be launched. Weeks more of waiting ran into months. Where was the car? What had happened to it? Its unexplained nonappearance became news in the trade journals and then in the papers.

For a second time in his life Ford couldn't have sold out in Wall Street for five cents on the dollar.

At length I went to Dearborn to find out what was wrong. The only lucid person there was Cameron.

He said: "I can make it simple as a statement of fact. But the facts are badly involved. We are dealing here with two very different men, one the inventor and one the manufacturer; both of them Mr. Ford. Formerly by the grace of God they had managed to come out at about the same place at the same time. This time the inventor is so far ahead of the manufacturer that we are all going crazy."

"Well, specifically, what?"

"The engine, for one thing. It's going to be an eight-cylinder V engine, as you probably know. For everybody else, for the Cadillac, it's good enough to cast a V engine block in two pieces and bolt them together.

71

That's not good enough for Mr. Ford. He says it has to be cast all in one piece. Our foundry men kept telling him it couldn't be done. He said they had to do it. I think at first he didn't know himself how it could be done, else he would have told them. That went on for weeks. Then one day he went into the foundry and did it with his own hands. Now we've got an eight-cylinder V engine block in one piece, which is something nobody else ever had, but what will happen next we don't know."

"That's wonderful advertising copy," I said. "Why not take pages of newspaper space and tell the story just that way? It will keep everybody waiting patiently."

"No," he said. "I know it's good copy. But we don't do things that way."

When at last the wonderful V-8 appeared it was the finest car Ford had ever made. Moreover, the design of it was not permitted to freeze. Year after year it was improved, if only in appearance. A new and strange kind of expert had been admitted to the Ford premises —one who could not be told by a Ford mechanic, "You do it our way." It was the industrial designer. Styling was as important as the engine.

Yet for all that, the Ford Motor Company's preeminence was lost. The V-8 could not restore it to first place.

The motor industry by this time was grown up. All

cars were good. Nobody could afford to make a poor one.

6

FOR grand mechanics it was twilight time. Engineers, scientists and technicians were taking over. General Motors had provided itself with one of the finest research laboratories in the world. Chrysler followed.

At Dearborn there was an engineering laboratory. Ford said of it: "We do nothing at all in what is sometimes ambitiously called research, except as it relates to our single object, which is making motors and putting them on wheels. In our engineering laboratory we are equipped to do almost anything we care to do, but our method is the Edison method of trial and error. . . ."

The boss mechanic speaking. Science is all right. But only a mechanic could have made Model T.

What made the Ford world so fabulous was not the car. All the time there were other and better cars, even from the beginning; and his was by no means the beginning.

One day in the engineering laboratory we happened to pass through his private shop—a mechanic's dream come true. He reached under the bench and dragged into the light his most precious relic.

"That's it," he said.

It was the first Ford car—a buggy box mounted on

73

four bicycle wheels, with some tiny machinery under the seat. He was seven years of nights making it, while holding a job as engineer in the powerhouse of the Edison Illuminating Company of Detroit. As he identified the bits and pieces of scrap it was made of—engine cylinders from a steam exhaust pipe, wheel hubs from railroad washers, and so on—he remembered driving it for the first time by the light of a lantern in the middle of a rainy night, how he had got from the mayor of Detroit a special permit to appear on the streets with it in daylight, and how when it stalled, as it sometimes did, he would chain it to a lamppost for fear somebody would make off with it before he could get back with repairs. The drive was a little leather belt, which perhaps had a better bite in the rain that first night. He could go only forward, but it would go, and it got him home, where Mrs. Ford was waiting with an umbrella.

"It would go now," he said, "if they hadn't been taking souvenirs off."

Then he pushed it back, saying: "That's what we beat the Selden patents with."

You may not remember. Selden was an obscure patent lawyer. He waited until the motor industry was already big and then turned up with sleeping patents that seemed to cover any automobile with an internal-combustion engine. He formed a licensing organization and notified all the makers of that kind of car to come in and settle on a royalty basis. One motor company

74

resisted and was beaten in court, whereupon there was created the Association of Licensed Automobile Manufacturers, all paying tribute for the right to use the Selden patents. The royalty was $1\frac{1}{2}$ per cent of their gross sales, and that was Golconda for Selden, who never in his life had tried to make an automobile.

Ford alone stood out. The Selden people took him to court and threatened also to hold every individual buyer of a Ford car liable for patent infringement. Ford thereupon offered with every Ford car a bond to protect the buyer. It became a celebrated matter and put Ford in the popular position of fighting the black powers of Wall Street. The first decision went against him. He appealed to a higher court and won.

It was true, as he said, that he won with that relic he had just pushed back under the bench. The interesting fact is, however, that although he stood alone and won alone, the decision of the court that delivered him delivered also the entire motor industry from the Selden trap. That was so because all automobiles with the internal-combustion engine were based on one and the same principle. If Ford was not infringing the Selden patents neither was anybody else.

All of which means simply that in the first Ford car there was no new principle, nothing that others did not know too and were already doing. It was a mechanic's achievement, not an original invention. And so it was in the next one and the next one and in all the millions of

Ford cars that followed. There was not in any of them a new basic principle. What his competitors learned and borrowed from him was nothing from the car itself.

7

AFTER the car, the next two pieces from the whimsy of the jigsaw were those named the time and the idea.

They go naturally together. No great success can be wrong in time. How often do we say of a brilliant man who has failed that he was before his time? Thirty years sooner both Ford and his Model T would have been too soon; thirty years later they would have been too late.

The fantasy of a horseless carriage was very old. In the *Iliad* you find Vulcan making for the gods wheeled vehicles that moved by an invisible force. Or you will find it in Ezekiel 1:15, when the angels appeared on wheels, and it was "as it were a wheel in the middle of a wheel," so that "when those went *these* went and when those stood *these* stood," this being the first vision of what happens in the transmission and differential mechanisms of your automobile. Nahum prophesied that "chariots shall rage in the streets and they shall jostle one against another in the broadways."

For twenty centuries men dreamed dreams, made drawings and fashioned models of self-propelled vehicles. They were all before their time.

The modern automobile was not possible without a marvelous advance in the mechanical arts, a science of metallurgy, a science of chemistry, precision tools, experience with the behavior of explosive gases, vulcanized rubber, the electric spark, petroleum for the fuel of the internal-combustion engine and oil for the lubrication of its parts.

At a point of time, say about 1880, all of these prerequisites began coming together in a rush in one field of free knowledge. It was then certain that in a little while many inventive minds would be working on parallel lines toward sudden realization of a very old dream. That is why it is impossible to say who invented what now we call the automobile, deriving its power from the internal-combustion engine.

Many people may have forgotten that it ever had any other kind of engine. The natural motive power seemed at first to be steam and some inventors clung to it in an obstinate manner. Then electric power was tried. During the first twenty years of the motor age steam, electricity and gas were in competition; each had its partisans. As late as 1897 the outcome was still in doubt. The day of the horseless carriage was arriving. Almost anybody could see that. But what would its motive power be? When in that year Thomas A. Edison said that the city streets would soon be full of vehicles driven by motors, he was asked if the power would be electricity, and he was expected to say yes because electricity was his obsession.

But he said: "I don't think so. As it looks at present, it is more likely that they will be run by gasoline or naphtha motors."

77

Edison and Ford met for the first time at a dinner of electricity people, Ford attending as chief engineer of the Edison Illuminating Company of Detroit. He was then building his first car and he explained his little internal-combustion engine to Edison, who said: "That's it, young man. You are on the right line. Don't let anybody throw you off."

Edison was right. The internal-combustion engine became the universal power of the automobile, here and everywhere else. In retrospect this may seem a little strange, because in mechanical theory the steam engine was much more efficient. Indeed, a mechanical engineer confronted for the first time with a blueprint of the internal-combustion engine with its silly poppet valves would be bound to say: "I suppose it would run. I can't imagine it would ever be efficient." The difficulties that had to be overcome to make it efficient were enormous. Its success was owing partly to the incentive of difficulty, which caused a vast amount of thought to become focused on it—since men do react that way—and partly to the marvelous and unpredictable availability of gasoline as motor fuel.

8

I T W A S not only that the materials and the knowledge became all at once present in time; there was what might be called a psychological dimension. The automobile itself was right in time. The mood of the people was restive and adventurous. They were in love with movement and speed and all in a great hurry to be somewhere and do something.

"Everybody," said Ford, "wants to be someplace he ain't. As soon as he gets there he wants to go right back."

Moreover, they were beginning to understand mechanical power as no people had ever understood it before.

If you could put into their individual hands a simple, complete and self-contained means of swift transportation, at a price they could afford to pay, the demand would be insatiable.

That is what Ford saw. That is what he meant when he said: "I will build a motor car for the great multitude." It was the magnificent and controlling idea of his life, and it was *not the idea of a mechanic.*

In twenty years it changed the habits and ways of thinking of an entire people and had, moreover, significant social consequences. Until then the automobile had been a plaything for the rich. Before Model T, Woodrow Wilson, speaking from his Princeton pulpit, had said that as a "new symbol of wealth's arrogance" the automobile was creating socialism in the hearts of the people. How different when anybody could own an automobile—and one that could keep going under conditions that often stopped the rich man's car.

Thus by a fortuitous running together of many things it was a time when the greatest unsatisfied want in the country was for an everyman's automobile. It might have been something else; in that case, given a Ford, the Model T would have been something else.

Ford once said: "The automobile is not what you see. Think of it as just a way of using power. Our civilization, such as it is, rests on cheap and convenient power."

After a day at River Rouge with Sorensen we came at twilight to his private office, which was a kind of watch tower on stilts, and at the top of the steps we stopped and stood there looking down on one of the stupendous industrial scenes of the world. He was the production manager and a genius at it.

He said: "You know, that isn't just automobiles. It might be anything else that people wanted enough of. It's the way of making it, the automobile or anything else."

But it *was* the automobile that people were then wanting enough of, and Ford's way of making it so revolutionized industrial method that the cost of making all cars was amazingly reduced. The automobile became therefore a necessary convenience of life, and by the time Model T had gone out of style it was possible for people to choose among a number of others. Yet this was true only because the entire motor industry had been obliged by the fact of fifteen million Model T's.

FOUR

THE MAD WAY

A T RIVER ROUGE, where the empire came of age, the hierarchy assumed its perfect form. Ford was god, Sorensen was satan and Cameron was pope. They communicated with one another in a language that only seemed to be made up of words. The meaning was in what they understood. Nothing was too strange to happen.

Ford had the kind of feeling for statistics that most people have for snakes, even friendly snakes. "Too many figures," he said, "make your head swell up like a drum." Nevertheless they persuaded him to let them make a few figures just to prove how useful they might be, only a few. He had forgotten all about it when one day a year later he stood rigid with bewilderment on the threshold of a large room full of computing machines, tabulating typewriters, mimeograph equipment, people drawing lines on large sheets of quad-ruled paper, and some colored charts on the walls. He beckoned to a person who looked up, and said to him:

"What's this?"

The startled person said: "This is our Statistical Department, Mr. Ford."

He stared for a moment with the look of one trying to remember something, then turned and walked away. In the yard he found Sorensen.

"Did I hear you say you needed some space?"

Sorensen said: "I need space like hell."

Ford said: "In that corner on the second floor where I'm pointing there is a big room. I just now happened to look into it. A lot of people making figures. You can have that space if you will go and take it."

Sorensen called two men to come in a hurry with crowbars, armed himself with a blunt instrument, and the three of them, descending upon the statistical department, wrecked it down to the floor, computing machines, typewriters, desks, everything. The terrified statisticians scattered and went home, only understanding that their department had been destroyed by an act of Providence. Sorensen sent the debris to the junk heap and moved in.

It would take Cameron to tell you why this was a perfectly rational piece of behavior. Mr. Ford, who in the first place had been persuaded against his judgment, found a large bureau growing on his premises. He knew the nature of bureaus. They grow like demon weeds. If you say, "Cut it down to half size," it will be obediently cut down; but when you come to look at it a year later it will be twice as big. The only way to control it, therefore, is to kill it. And that is what

82

Sorensen knew. Cameron would add: "Moreover, Mr. Ford thinks the statistician's facts are dead before they are written down. He says that by the time anyone has assembled a large collection of facts on any subject their value has so changed that they are a record of the past and useless, even dangerous, as guides to the future. The only facts he cares about are the facts he finds as he moves forward."

It was at River Rouge that what was called the Ford method came to marvelous fruition. All the principles had been worked out. Although Ford said, "Fortunately, we inherited no traditions and are not founding any," nevertheless he was founding one, and on second thought he added: "If we have a tradition it is this: Everything can always be done faster and better. That pressing always to do work better and faster serves nearly every factory problem."

No superintendent had to think of anything else. He would be wasting his time if he did. At the end of each day he divided the output of his department by the number of workers employed, and that was his score. If his score was good everything else would come out right.

And it was at River Rouge that for the first time Ford had the leisure to think in a conscious manner, to look back at what he had done without thinking and to rationalize it in theory. Then, finding the clear words for it, he pronounced this dictum:

"The new method must produce the profit. Never

cheapen the product. Never cheapen the wage. Never overcharge the public. Put your brains into the method, more brains, and still more."

Until we come to the piece named X, this will stand as the secret of the greatest individual profit maker of his age, or of any age so far.

Note that in this dictum he says *new* method. Let the new method produce the profit. Yet the fact is that the Ford method, like the Model T car, had nothing radically new in it, nothing that somebody else had not already thought of.

Before Fordism there was Taylorism. Frederick W. Taylor was the John the Baptist of scientific management. The original principles that were afterward so amazingly demonstrated by Ford were being taught by Taylor in textbooks, in lectures and in practice, long before there was a Ford Motor Company. Taylor was the revolutionary thinker; Ford was the revolutionist in action. The Ford assembly line was the first of its kind ever installed in the world, but the idea came in a general way from the overhead trolley that the Chicago packers use in dressing beef, where each butcher in turn takes one part of the carcass and then pushes it on to the next butcher, who takes another part, and so on, until there is nothing left of it. This you might call a disassembly line. Ford turned it upside down to make the first assembly line on which a thing is built up, not dismembered.

What made the Ford method epochal was not discovery but the imagination, the ingenuity, the excitement and the total logic with which the principles of scientific management were applied. Of general principles, Ford said he knew only two, namely:

(1) That a man should never have to take more than one step if it could possibly be avoided, which meant simply that the man stood still and the work moved, and,

(2) That no man should ever need to stoop over, which meant that his work should be brought to him waist-high.

Yet he is speaking there of practice, not principles.

Why should a man never take more than one step? Because steps take time. "Save ten steps a day for each of twelve thousand employees," Ford said, "and you will have saved fifty miles of wasted motion and misspent energy. The undirected worker spends more of his time walking about for materials and tools than he does in working. Pedestrianism cannot be highly paid."

And why should a man never stoop? Because it takes time and energy to stoop and lift, and, said Ford, "We think of time as human energy." That brings him closer to it.

In the last term there is but one principle, and that is to overcome time.

The cost of transforming raw materials into useful forms may be reduced to that one term—time. Labor is time. Machines are time. Raw materials are time. Visibly, the industrial process consists in passing raw materials through hands and machines. Actually, it consists only in passing them through time. The use of the machine is to enable you to pass them faster through time. A lone craftsman may spend a lifetime making one exquisite watch. What is it worth? It is worth his whole lifetime, provided a rich man can be found with the whim to buy it for no better reason than to be able to say that he carries one man's lifetime in his vest pocket.

2

ONE of the contradictions is that the Ford car came first and the Ford method afterward. For nearly ten years the Ford car was built as every other car was built. That is to say, it was built like a house. The chassis was the foundation. There it stood on one spot and never moved until the car was finished, with mechanics, helpers and stock runners bringing things to it, one part at a time.

That would be the cheapest way to build a few cars. The very cheapest way to build one car would be to build it entirely by hand, with a few simple tools—a lathe, a drill press, anvil, forge and vise—as Ford built his first car; and still it was a costly car because it took him seven years to do it. For one car or for a few cars you could not afford to spend millions of dollars for automatic lathes and milling machines, multiple drill presses that make twenty holes at once in four different directions at the touch of a red button, or ten-ton forging hammers that react with diabolic energy when you step lightly on their bunions.

The Ford Motor Company had success by the mane, "Watch the Fords Go By" was a vaunting advertising line on the billboards and in animated electric signs against the sky by night, other automobile makers were gnashing their teeth for envy and the output of Model T's was ten thousand a year—when Ford began to hear voices.

He dared not tell what they said to him. It was too fantastic.

They said: "Not thousands. Millions! Automobiles by the million. The people want them, if only you can make them."

He looked at his shop. It was still like any other automobile shop of that time. Each one in its own way was a little pandemonium. Each new car was witness that purpose enough will somehow overcome confusion to bring its ends to pass. But in that way you could never make automobiles by the million. In the first place, you never could find the skilled mechanics. Secondly, provided you could find them, you would not be able to manage them. How could you manage maybe a million skilled mechanics in one plant?

The first fact therefore was that if you were going to build automobiles by the million you would have to do it with unskilled labor, of which there was always plenty. Then you would have to have not only many, many more machines; you would have to revolutionize

87

your way of thinking about the machine. Actually you could not dispense with skill; but you could build skill into the machine—automatic, unerring skill. A man of very ordinary intelligence could mind such a machine, because he would have only to fill its maw according to a formula and then activate it by pulling a lever or stepping on a treadle, all with a few disciplined motions of his hands and feet, the fewer the better. And he could be trained to do that in a few hours.

What followed logically was an extreme problem of internal transportation—how to move the material to the men at the machines and away from them in a continuous flow. The answer to that was the conveyer belt.

Many engineers and highly skilled mechanics would be needed of course to design and build the machines— strange and specialized machines, new-purpose machines, such machines as the regular machine builders had never heard of, could hardly imagine at all, and sometimes were loath to build on Ford designs, thinking they would not work. What they learned was that if you take thought enough you can build a machine to blow soap bubbles.

A Ford man going to and fro in the world was expected to keep his eyes alert for any new wrinkle in machine craft that could be copied or adapted. Anyone who could think of a new machine or of a better way to make an old one work was king for a day.

You will realize that the Ford way could not have been thought out all at once. It wasn't. There were too

88

many unexpected complications; the solution of one difficulty brought unexpected problems into view. It had to grow by trial and error. The idea of it was constant, obsessionary and extravagant; the pressure behind it was terrific. If a thing worked on a trial scale it was immediately adopted on a large scale. Almost overnight any whole section of the plant might be turned out to make room for it.

Moving the work to the man, and from one machine to another, by gravity slides and conveyor belts, with the man standing still, was first tried on what are called subassemblies.

The engine is an example of subassembly. The complete engine as a thing in itself, with several hundred parts, some heavy and some as delicate as watch parts, is all put together before it arrives at the chassis to take its place in the automobile. That would be the same if one mechanic were building an automobile entirely by hand. Naturally he would assemble the engine on the bench before putting it on the chassis.

In the old way one man assembled the entire Ford engine, walking round and round it until it was finished. In the new way, what that one man did was broken down into eighty-four separate operations, one man to each operation, all eighty-four of them standing still, with the work moving past them waist-high, each man having just time enough to do his one thing. Where formerly only one man touched the engine, now eighty-four act upon it in sequence, but you do not have now eighty-

89

four men where before you had one. What happens is that whereas before it took eighty-four men to assemble eighty-four engines, now eighty-four men assemble 252 engines, or three times as many.

Another example of subassembly was the flywheel magneto, a feature of the Model T that now is extinct. When one man did the whole job the time was twenty minutes. When the job was broken down into thirty-nine operations, with the men standing still and the work moving past them, the time was reduced to seven minutes.

The first result of speeding up the subassemblies in this manner was to confound confusion. Each subassembly line was a rising stream and there was no river to take the flood. There stood the chassis still, in the middle of the floor, with everybody running around it, everybody bringing something to it, until somehow a finished automobile should appear; so that of course the faster the subassemblies arrived—the engine, the flywheel magneto, the transmission, the rear axle differential, and so on—the madder the disorder was.

Then a natural thought presented itself. *The chassis had to move!*

That may seem now to have been a very simple translation of what they already knew into its logical next dimension, and yet what it did was to call out of the dimness a mighty revolution of practice. The last secret of mass production was discovered.

First they got a windlass and 250 feet of rope and

dragged the chassis slowly along the floor. Everything had been timed and arranged beforehand. Parts and subassemblies were piled along the way, so that the right part and the right subassembly would be there within arm's reach, just as the chassis arrived, and the workers either walked with the chassis or rode it, doing their work as they moved, keeping their tools in their hands.

That was a capital day. Never before had a car been assembled in less than twelve hours and twenty-eight minutes. This one at the end of the rope was assembled in five hours and fifty minutes.

Well, if that could be done with one chassis at a time, why not tie eight or ten to the end of the rope? That was tried. The speed of the windlass was increased. The parts and subassemblies along the way were delivered waist-high, the easier to be picked up, and each man's operation was further simplified. By these improvements the time required to assemble a car was squeezed again. So now there began to be a river for the subassembly streams to flow into and everybody was happy.

Until one day the rope broke; the automobiles at the end of it, building as they moved, piled up in a dead heap.

They threw away the windlass and rope and sat down to think. What they thought of was a power-driven endless conveyer belt, flush with the floor, like an escalator running on the level. It was wide enough to hold not only the chassis but workers on both sides of it, so that

91

the workers and the automobile moved together, each worker doing his specialized bit of work, then stepping back a few paces to do it again to the next car, in a string of forty-five.

As Ford described it, the line moved six feet a minute. There were forty-five building stations, at each of which something was added to the moving car. The first man fastened four mudguard brackets to the chassis frame; the engine arrived at the tenth station, and so on. Some men did only one or two small operations, others more. The man who placed a part did not always fasten it. The part might not be fully in place until several stations later. The man who put in a bolt might not put on the nut; the man who put on the nut might not tighten it. At station thirty-four the engine got its gasoline; it had previously had lubrication. At station forty-four the radiator was filled with water, and at station forty-five the engine started. Then the car moved away under its own power.

On that first conveyer belt the time required to assemble an automobile was reduced to ninety-three minutes—from twelve hours and twenty-eight minutes.

This made such a raging river through the middle of the shop that the subassembly lines began to run dry. So they had to be raised higher and higher and more were added, and the work everywhere was subdivided again and again to a point at which each operation was incredibly simplified.

"With the result," said Ford, "that the necessity for

92

thought on the part of the worker is reduced to a minimum. He does, if it is possible, only one thing with one movement."

There seemed to be no limit to how far you could go in that direction. Ford overhauled his fantasy of a car a minute. It did not stop there. Five years later a Model T was appearing every ten seconds of the working day. That was mass production. In his passion for it Ford called it the New Messiah. Everything to satisfy material human wants could be produced in that way, and if everything were, then man for the first time could have both plenty without end and the leisure to consume it.

His feud with time was relentless. As some people at a glance see four-leaf clovers in the grass, so in his marginal vision as he walked through the shop he could see waste of labor, energy and materials, all three representing time. It might be something he himself had not noticed yesterday.

One day he passed the men who were testing the engine. He turned back suddenly and asked one of them: "Why do we do that?" The man was struck dumb. He did not understand that Ford was putting the question not to him but to himself. Always the Ford engine, like every other engine, was put on a block and tested under its own power before being installed in the automobile. It was standard practice. Ford left the man staring, went straight to his engineers and said: "The only reason we make a trial run of the engine is we are not

93

sure we made it right. Let's make sure of that and stop this testing."

After that the Ford engine came alive in the automobile as it drove off the end of the assembly line.

3

PARTURITION in the mechanical kingdom is a sweet and charming event, essentially marvelous, and yet so blurred by dull-witted familiarity that few of us ever see it in the pure light of wonder. It happens that in the automobile engine you cannot see it at all. The action is concealed. But to have seen it, for example, in the case of a steam locomotive, with all the action visible, is something to remember.

That magnificent animal now is doomed by evolution and will presently survive only in museums, like lions in the zoo. It begins with white lines on dark paper—the flat blueprints. Skilled mechanics labor for months to raise it to the third dimension. Then at last there it is, complete, standing on a track of wheels so that it may run without moving, and still inanimate. Movement is unknown to it.

A high-pressure steam line is attached; a valve is turned. The first sign of life is a tremor of astonishment; then a gasp and a half-strangled cough. The big drive wheels start to revolve, hesitate, stagger slightly, and you think of a newborn calf taking its first sprawling steps; they make one revolution, stumble again, then

94

begin to turn smoothly, faster and faster, until they find their rhythm.

So an engine comes alive. Any engine. Millions a day come alive in the world, and although the birth rate is recorded statistically by the economists, to tell us how fast our race of mechanical slaves is propagating itself, it is not otherwise regarded.

But there was a time when the first engine—the very first one—clumsily moved. Next to the dawn of animal life, that was the miracle most pregnant and most brooding in all the apocalyptic story of the earth.

Whence came the engine? Who makes it? We seem to be sure that God does not make it. God makes the elephant. The elephant therefore belongs to the mystery of life. It is what we call a natural fact. By the hand of man, issuing from the creative power of his imagination, come an engine that can fly elephants through the firmament; and yet we say there is nothing mysterious about the engine. It is an artificial fact.

We think it not at all mysterious that engines procreate engines. Without engines we could not have engines. We have discovered a law of evolution in the animal world, and that is mysterious; but engines evolve from lower to higher forms much faster than anything in the animal world. Engines today are of different kinds and species and much less like the engines of one hundred years ago than people are like monkeys, after aeons of time. Physicists can tell you why engines run.

95

They found it out afterward. It is because gases behave
in a certain way. If you ask them why gases behave in
a certain way they cannot tell you, nor can anyone
explain why the engine is the only form of absolute
truth in the possession of mankind.

Anyhow, with engines coming alive faster than one
a minute on his assembly lines, and time screaming for
mercy on the banks of the River Rouge, Ford began to
look in new directions for greater occasions to pursue
his feud.

4

BY THIS time the Ford Motor Company did much
more than to fabricate automobiles. It had become a
vast integrated manufacturing empire, going all the
way back to the sources of raw materials, such as to
get ore from its own iron mines, fuel from its own coal
mines, wood from its own forests, rubber from its own
plantations, chemicals from its own vats, fabrics from
its own looms—and was potentially self-contained. Although it continued to buy enormously from suppliers
and contractors when there was advantage in it, still it
was ready to manufacture for itself anything that was
needed to make an automobile, and sometimes made
things just to see if it could, like rubber tires and glass
for windshields, without intending really to go into
either the rubber tire or the glass business, unless the
tire and glass makers got too proud with their prices.

As he looked in these new directions all he could see

96

was a chaos of waste. Nobody doing anything the Ford way.

The worst wasters of all were the railroads. They wasted not only their own time but Ford time, which was unforgivable. Their inefficiency scandalized him. Railroad people, he said, had been so long at war with their employees and with the public that the purpose of railways was sometimes forgotten. When they were unable to handle their traffic properly the only thing they could think of was to borrow more money to increase their facilities. The right way would be first to make sure they were using their facilities to the utmost, and if they did that they might find that it was not necessary to increase them at all.

He had tried to show them how. Formerly he shipped automobiles as everybody else did, whole, and seven to a freight car. The first time he made as many as one thousand cars in a day and tried to ship them he created the worst traffic jam Detroit had ever seen. What would it be like when he wanted to ship twice that many?

So he began to ship them knocked down, to be assembled at the branch plants; and that way he could get one hundred and thirty in one freight car. He went much further. More and more the branch plants all over the country assembled the cars and did also some manufacturing, so that only the subassemblies and the bits and pieces went out from Detroit, and these packed and crated with such geometric precision that a loaded freight car was as full as an eggshell.

97

But for a living industrial process that required the oxygen of a continuous and invariable flow of materials, incoming freight was a nightmare. It was uncertain, whimsical, generally tardy and in the best case too slow, only for the reason that railroads were run like that. "For a railroad to deliver in ten days what it might deliver in five is grand larceny," he said; and if it delivered in five days its facilities would be doubled.

He had found that in stockpiles and warehouses he had $200,000,000 of capital tied up, dead capital in raw materials and finished automobiles, all as insurance against the aberrations of railroad transportation. He hated stockpiles and warehouses. He perceived that the time cost in manufacturing began the moment the raw material was separated from the earth and continued until the finished product was delivered to the consumer. Having on hand twice as much material as was needed —which was only another way of saying twice as much stored human labor as was needed—was precisely the same as hiring two men to do the job of one, and hiring two men to do the job of one was a crime.

So he resolved to abolish stockpiles and tear down his warehouses. Five years later, when that feud was won, he found that in that time the extension of the business, which had been very great, had all been paid for with money that before would have been idle in piles of iron, steel, coal, or in finished automobiles. Now he did not own or use a single warehouse.

How did he do it?

First was created a Ford Traffic Department that became the day-and-night torment of the railroad people. From the moment a car of Ford freight started from anywhere, until it arrived, it was a red ant in their pants. On its departure a Ford man wired in its number. At the first junction or breaking point there was another Ford man to check its arrival, to see that it got on its way again, and to report it by wire; and so at the next point and the next one, until it arrived in home territory, and there again was a Ford man to pick it up and see it to the unloading platform. There was a kind of military precision about it. If anywhere on the map, day or night, a car loaded with Ford freight was an hour late the Ford Traffic Department knew it and there was hell to pay. Ford freight was nothing a railroad could afford to lose.

For ore there was a fleet of Ford boats running from the head of the Great Lakes to Detroit—the engine rooms finished in gray and white with all nickel-plated trim, the crew's quarters finished in hardwood, a shower bath for each man—and the story of the ore was as follows: 64990

Forty-eight hours down the Lakes from Marquette the ore boat docks at Fordson on the River Rouge at 8 A.M., Monday. Ten minutes later its cargo is moving toward the High Line and becomes part of a charge for the blast furnace. By noon Tuesday, the ore has been reduced to iron, mixed with other iron in the foundry cupolas, and cast. Thereupon follow fifty-eight opera-

99

tions, which are performed in fifty-five minutes. By three o'clock in the afternoon the motor has been finished and started off in a freight car to a branch for assembly into a finished car. Say that it reaches the branch plant so that it may be put into the assembly line at eight o'clock Wednesday morning. By noon the car will be on the road in the possession of its owner. If the motor, instead of being sent to a branch plant, goes into the assembly line for the Detroit district, then the completed car will be delivered before five o'clock Tuesday afternoon instead of at noon Wednesday.

From ore on the dock to the finished car in sixteen working hours.

When the stockpiles had vanished and the last warehouse had been torn down, the production cycle, that is, the elapsed time from the moment the ore was separated from the earth at the mine to the appearance of the finished automobile, had been reduced from fourteen days to three days and nine hours.

A further step was the ocean-going and coastwise vessel, designed, like a one-purpose machine, for Ford cargo only, with special racks, so that nothing had to be crated. The saving on crating alone might be as much as twenty thousand dollars a trip.

Yet the main thing was time. A Ford ship was held to schedule like a railroad passenger train, and was limited to twenty-four hours in port, because if a ship was held a couple of weeks in port, unloading and loading, the loss would probably be greater than the total

100

wages for a year. The total of wages paid on a ship was not very important. The important thing was to see that you got full use out of the big investment, namely, the ship.

Time was money and time loved to be wasted. Idle money was time and money loved to be idle. To tolerate this evil association was Ford's idea of mortal economic sin.

"From time waste," he said, "there can be no salvage. It is the easiest of all waste and the hardest to correct because it does not litter the floor."

FIVE

THE MAGIC LEVER

T H E X piece comes here. A small mind's-eye etching may help to get it right side up.

This is something you might see in New England. On a fine hill is the dilapidation of what was once a rich man's house. In the valley below it the elements are gnawing at what is left of an abandoned textile mill and scattered around are some small dwellings falling apart. There is nowhere a sign of human activity. It is one of industry's deserted villages, with no one to sing its elegy. Yet elsewhere, even in this valley, the textile industry is flourishing.

What happened here? The mill in the valley built the house on the hill, and then both the mill and the house died. Simply, the owner, to build his house, took too much out of the mill. He thought what he took was profit. He was wrong. The penalty of mistaking it for profit was that he lost everything, both his income and his capital, and lost, moreover, that sense of satisfaction that may come from providing a livelihood for maybe hundreds of mill workers.

This therefore was the job that devoured itself.

What should he have done with what he thought was profit? He should have put it back. He should have used the money to buy the latest and most efficient textile machinery, to improve his methods of manufacture, to hire the talent that could design new fabrics and the engineers who could have told how to reduce his costs. His profits would have increased, and still he should not have taken them out. Instead he should have raised wages in order to get better workers, and then he should have reduced his selling prices to attract more customers, thereby increasing the volume of his business, which of course would have obliged him to enlarge the mill. What was left after all that he might call profit, and although he might have had to wait for his grand house, there would have been a growing and prosperous textile business in the valley.

Does it follow that profit is an illusory thing? Not at all.

As there is a law of compound interest so there is a law of compound profit.

Compound interest on a dollar invested at 5 per cent in the time of Caesar would now be more money than there is in the whole world. A thousand nabobs could not spend it. So with profit. If instead of taking it out you put it back you get richer and richer. If the man on that New England hill had put his profits back, more and more, he might have become the richest textile manufacturer in New England, or in the whole world, with earnings at the latter end so large that the cost of a palatial dwelling could have been no more than a thimbleful.

This is what Ford did. He dispraised the profit motive.

Any business that thought first of earning a fixed dividend was bound to fail. Either profits would come from doing the job well or they would not come at all. A properly conducted business could not fail to return a profit.

Then he made this cryptic saying: "A business absolutely devoted to service will have only one worry about profits. *They will be embarrassingly large.*"

The growth of the Ford Motor Company was of this order:

To build the first million cars took nearly twenty years.

To build the next four million took six years.

To build the next five million took only three years, and the capacity then was two million cars a year.

All of that growth, from a rude frame building where a few perspiring mechanics assembled eight or ten cars a day to a self-contained empire with a capacity of two million cars a year—the industrial monster on the River Rouge, plants all over the world, mines and plantations and forests and ships, and even a railroad of its own —all of this had been bought and paid for out of earnings. The original capital was twenty-eight thousand

104

dollars ; and never in its life did the Ford Motor Company borrow a dollar.

As he put the earnings back, with the passion of a parlay gambler, he kept saying it was the public's money, not his. The public provided the capital, he said, not by way of buying Ford stock or Ford bonds but as it bought more and more Ford cars.

Each year there had been a profit. Nearly all of it had gone back into the business to provide the means further to reduce the cost of making a car. But it was not an investment on which the Ford Motor Company was entitled to receive interest.

That money, he believed, was the public's money. As the public, having confidence in him, bought his product, so it provided his capital. Where else could the money have come from, since he did not borrow it? He felt he had no right to charge the public interest on its own money.

When earnings were used to buy a mine, for example, the profit from the mine belonged not to the company but to the public.

In raw materials there was a profit. A coal profit, a limestone profit, an ore profit, a lumber profit, a transportation profit, and so on. Was the manufacturer justified in collecting for himself each one of these profits and adding it to the profit he received for turning raw materials into articles of use? If he was a true businessman, operating on the principle of service, he

105

abolished all subsidiary profits and gave the customer the benefit of them.

And what was true of a mine was true even of a machine bought out of earnings. That machine did not belong either to the man who bought it or to the man who operated it, but to the public. Neither the workmen nor the owner could get a profit from the machine except as it benefited the public.

2

HIS way with profits appears to have proceeded at first from intuition. Then he found that it worked. The theory came later, and the theory was this: If an article costs a dollar less to produce, and the dollar comes off the price, the result is that more people are able to buy. More buyers make a still larger business. A larger business still further reduces the cost, which in turn increases the business again. If, on the other hand, the one dollar saved is added to the manufacturer's profit, the price to the consumer remaining the same, there will be no change in the volume of business. If the dollar saved is added to wages, there will be no change in the volume of business. But from sharing the profit with the public comes an immediate and great public benefit. There is a stimulating effect on the business, prices go lower, business increases, more men are employed, wages increase, profits rise.

The return to the public was in the price of the car.

The first Model T sold for $1,200. During its life-time it sold as low as $295.

A Ford automobile for $295 was certainly the cheap-est satisfaction of a material human want that ever appeared in the world.

His enthusiasm for cutting the price kept his engi-neers and managers in a state of delirium. Once he cut it when the demand was already running far in excess of the plant's utmost capacity; and the only sane reason he could give for doing that was that the profits were awful.

"A business that makes too much profit," he said, "disappears almost as quickly as one that operates at a loss."

At that time he made the following statement to the press: "We could easily have maintained our price for this year and cleaned up $60,000,000 to $75,000,000, but I do not think it would be right to do so. We cut prices and are now clearing $2,000,000 to $2,500,000 a month, which is all any firm ought to make, maybe more, unless the money is to be used for expansion. I have been fighting to hold down income right along."

Once he announced that if so many cars were sold in the year, every Ford buyer would get a refund, like a profit-sharing bonus, and every buyer did. There was some canniness in that. He knew that if his sales reached a certain volume his costs would be lower.

Sometimes he would set a price at which no profit was

visible—a price actually below cost, just to see if they could make it, and they always did.

The shoemaker who, on being asked how he determined the price of a pair of shoes, said, "First I make the shoes and then I charge how," stated the classic economic axiom. How else would you arrive at a price?

But Ford said the price came first. If you made the right price the cost would take care of itself.

That was paradox. Price before cost. No economist could have imagined cost as a function of price; and until four and four made five it couldn't be. Ford made it make sense in practice, and afterward he gave the theory of it, thus:

"When we first reduce the price to a point where, as we think, more sales will result, then we go ahead and try to meet the price. The new price will force the cost down. The more usual way is to calculate the cost and then set the price. That method may be scientific in the narrow sense; it is not scientific in the broad sense. What use is it to know the cost if it tells you that you cannot manufacture at a price at which the article can be sold?"

But more to the point was the fact that although one might know what the cost was, no one knew what the cost ought to be. One of the ways to discover what the cost ought to be was to name a price so low as to force everybody in the shop to the highest point of efficiency. The low price made you dig for profits. Ford said he had made more discoveries under this forced method than he could have made by any way of calculating costs beforehand.

In *My Life and Work* he said it another way: "Reducing prices is taken by the short-sighted to be the same as reducing the income of the business. It is very difficult to deal with that sort of mind. For instance, I was once asked when contemplating a reduction of eighty dollars a car, whether on a production of five hundred thousand cars this would not reduce the income of the company by forty million dollars. Of course, if one sold only five hundred thousand cars at the new price, the income would be reduced forty million dollars —which was an interesting mathematical calculation that had nothing to do with business. Old time business went on the doctrine that prices should be kept up to the highest point at which people would buy. Modern business has to take the opposite view." *

True to their race, his own minority stockholders had "that sort of mind." In the thirteenth year he resolved to be rid of them. Although he himself owned a majority of the stock and could do with the company almost as he would, nevertheless they worried him.

3

OF THE twelve original investors, who had put up twenty eight thousand dollars among them, five had sold out early, leaving seven. From their penny-ante

* *My Life and Work,* by Henry Ford. Copyright 1922 by Doubleday & Co., Inc.

bets on Ford these seven had all become millionaires. They were not active in the business, excepting one; they contributed nothing in the way of ideas. They regarded the Ford Motor Company simply "as a money-making machine."

The capital each one had put in at the beginning had been returned to him a thousand times; incredible as that was, still it was not enough, because on the visible earnings it might have been more. To all of them, Ford's way of putting the earnings back, instead of dividing them, was a kind of plowman's folly. The results so far had been amazing; that was so. Yet they held among them the uneasy feeling that he was a dangerous fantast, touched with megalomania. Riding with him was like moving at high velocity in a vehicle that could not stop. He said he could see the road ahead. They couldn't see it and they had only his word for it that he could. But they could all be immediately richer if only he would divide the earnings.

The cards were cut the day he set his heel in the marsh of the River Rouge and said: "We'll put it here." A few days later he announced that the Ford Motor Company had set its sights for an expansion program that would cost one hundred million dollars.

The minority stockholders turned pale. They very well knew where the money would come from. It would come out of earnings. And that would mean one hundred million less ever to be divided as profit.

The two most difficult minority stockholders were a

pair of hard Scots named Dodge—John and Horace
Dodge—brothers, who used to go every night to the
Detroit Athletic Club in long black coats, eat two steaks
just alike, mellow from monosyllables to utter silence,
then rise arm in arm and support each other on the way
to bed. A solemn ritual that came to be treated with a
kind of sentimental reverence.

They were marine engine builders at first, with a repu-
tation for the finest machine shop practice in Detroit.
They took the contract to make the first Ford engines,
from Ford's blueprints. There was supposed to be some
risk in the contract because the Ford Motor Company
had almost no capital, and to make the engine the
Dodge brothers had to buy new equipment. As a kind of
insurance they took one hundred shares of stock, not
for cash but on their promissory notes; and the notes
were paid off later out of earnings, so that in fact the
Dodge brothers put into the Ford Motor Company no
cash at all, nor, for that matter, did Ford. He didn't
have any. His contribution to the original capital was
his name, his work and his mechanical designs. But for
toughness, willingness and sheer love of martyrdom, the
Ford engines that came from the Dodge brothers' machine shop were the best that were ever made, and much
of the success of the first Ford cars was owing to that
fact.

The Ford contract turned out to be enormously prof-
itable for the Dodge brothers. It lasted ten years. When
Ford moved to the big Highland Park plant and began

111

to make his own engines it was terminated. But besides the profit they had made during ten years on the contract, the Dodge brothers still had the stock they had acquired in the beginning—the stock they bought with ten thousand dollars of self-liquidating promissory notes—and on that stock they had already received dividends of ten million dollars.

After Ford began to make his own engines they decided to go into the automobile business for themselves, and very successfully brought out the Dodge car, at a higher price than the Ford car. That was when one of the Dodges said, "Think how many Ford buyers would like to have a real automobile for a little more money." The only Ford car at that time was still Model T.

All of this was in the grain when Ford announced that he was going to spend one hundred million dollars of the company's earnings on the evidence of things unseen. His output at that time was half a million cars a year. His voices were telling him to make it a million a year—two million a year. And the voices were right.

John Dodge called Ford on the telephone and invited him to visit the Dodge plant, which Ford had never seen. Ford took along a witness. It was going to be a duel and somebody would get hurt. Both men understood that. For a while they talked warily of things they were not thinking about, as one mechanic to another, and as old friends besides, with specious amiability. John Dodge made the first feint. That was only to say he was sorry Ford had found it necessary to break with Jim Couzens.

Those were not innocent words.

From the beginning until just then James Couzens had been the great he-person in the Ford organization. His gifts were four—a genius for the role of ringmaster in the arena of business, an immense store of surplus energy, a terrible temper and leonine roaring pouches. He was a clerk in the office of the coal dealer Malcomson who was Ford's No. 1 backer, and Malcomson put him into the Ford Motor Company to watch the books. Couzens was a young believer. With nine hundred dollars of his own money, one hundred dollars of his sister's money and his promissory note for fifteen hundred dollars he bought twenty-five shares of the original stock. Almost from the first the understanding between Ford and Couzens was that of a brotherhood of two against the others. Their working relationship had a certain pattern. As the business grew in its fabulous way Couzens' place more and more was in the spotlight, which he loved, and Ford's place was in the background, where for a long time he preferred to be. Many were misled to think Couzens was in fact the king gear he seemed to be. Even some of the minority stockholders got that notion, and it was a comfort for them, for they knew Couzens to be a conservative at heart, no matter what he might say to the contrary; and so long as he was there, so long as he was the indispensable man on whom Ford relied for sound judgments, he could be trusted to exert a restraining influence.

Ford did nothing to hurt that little fable. It amused him to play up to it with acts of exaggerated deference. He would sometimes approach Couzens' door on tiptoe, with a finger on his lips, and whisper, "Is the old ogre in?" Yet when the break came it was like touching the end of a lighted cigarette to a piece of taut cotton twine. One morning Couzens delivered himself of an ultimatum, touching something unpopular Ford was going to say about World War I in his weekly, the Dearborn *Independent*. He said: "If that is printed, I quit." Ford said: "All right, Jim. You'd better go." After that Couzens was just another minority stockholder, with a mind more like theirs than like Ford's, and the Ford Motor Company went on as if nothing had happened.

Now here was John Dodge saying to Ford he was sorry that Jim Couzens had to go. What he meant was that it had been an act of folly for the Ford Motor Company to throw away the only braking mechanism it had.

Ford took it that way and replied lightly. It was a good thing, he said, for "now we can go ahead and do what we want to do."

"What are you going to do?" Dodge asked.

Ford said: "Double the plant, double the output and cut the price of the car in half."

Dodge said: "If you are going to do that and run

the business with no regard for the minority stockholders you ought to buy them out. We will sell you our stock right now."

Ford said he wasn't buying anybody's stock. He already owned a majority of it, and he would run the business as he pleased.

On that note the visit ended. No blood yet.

4

T H E next thing the seven minority stockholders heard from Ford was very bad news for their pockets. From then on, Ford told them, the Ford Motor Company would pay dividends of only $1,200,000 a year. Roughly, that was one tenth of what it had been paying; and they could take it or leave it. All earnings over that would be returned to the business.

The Dodge brothers went to court, seeking an order to compel Ford to distribute the Ford Motor Company's earnings to its stockholders; pending the outcome of the action they asked that the one-hundred-million-dollar expansion program be enjoined.

The trial was a transposed version of "Who Stole the Tarts?" Sense made nonsense and nonsense made sense and the sanity of language was imperiled.

Seven investors who had already got their capital back a thousand times were hurt and demanding relief because their dividends had been reduced to *60 per cent a year*.

The greatest profit maker of the age was in flight

115

from profits and always had been and that was how he made them.

A company might make awful profits in spite of itself. Its profits might get so big that it could not afford to distribute them.

The Mad Hatter said it all began with the twinkling of the tea.

"The twinkling of what?" said the king.

"It began with the tea," the Hatter replied.

"Of course, twinkling began with the tea," said the king. "Go on."

"I'm a poor man," the Hatter went on—

Ford said: "We don't seem able to keep profits down. It has been my policy to force the price of the car down as fast as increased production would permit."

The Dodge lawyer said: "Your conscience would not let you make such awful profits?"

Ford said: "I don't know that my conscience has anything to do with it."

The Dodge lawyer said: "Why did you say it wasn't right to make such awful profits if it wasn't your conscience?"

Ford said: "It isn't good business."

The Dodge lawyer said: "You started in to make money, didn't you? That was why the company was organized?"

Ford said: "I didn't give it much thought. The best way to make money in business is not to think too much about making it."

The Dodge lawyer said: "But you got a lot of money out of it, didn't you? And you still do, don't you?"

Ford said: "The money is not mine to do with as I please. The men who work with me have helped to create it. After they have had their wages and a share of the profits, it is my duty to take what remains and put it back into the industry to create more work for more men at higher wages."

The Dodge lawyer said: "Your controlling idea, since you have all the money *you* want, is to employ a great army of men at high wages, reduce the selling price so that a lot of people can buy a car cheap—give everybody a car who wants one?"

Ford said: "If I did all that the money would fall in my lap. I couldn't get away from it."

The Dodge lawyer wanted to know what Ford meant to do with the money he was withholding from his stockholders.

Ford said, for one thing, he was going to make castings direct from the ore at one melt. That would be a great saving.

The Dodge lawyer said: "Who is doing that now?"

Ford said: "Nobody."

The Dodge lawyer said: "And you are going to experiment with the Ford Company's money to do something nobody has even tried to do before?"

Ford said: "There wouldn't be any fun for us if we didn't try things people say we can't do."

The Dodge lawyer asked if it wouldn't be better to keep the money as a reserve against bad times.

Ford's lawyer made the interjection that if the money were paid out in dividends they wouldn't have it, either in the form of new assets or as a reserve against bad times.

Ford, looking over at John Dodge, said: "Maybe we could ask the stockholders to give the dividends back if we needed them. How about it, John?"

The court took refuge in arithmetic. The Ford Motor Company's profits that year had been above fifty-two million dollars, and Ford was proposing to give his stockholders hardly more than one fiftieth of them.

The court said: "It is not within the lawful power of a corporation to shape and conduct its affairs for the merely incidental benefit of shareholders and for the primary purpose of benefiting others."

And it ordered him to declare forthwith a dividend of $19,275,000. That one dividend was $688 for each one dollar of cash originally invested in the Ford Motor Company, or 68,800 per cent. On the par value of $100,000, which was the Ford Motor Company's original capitalization, it was a dividend of 19,275 per cent. Stated thus in percentages the figures are of course grotesque.

5

B U T the seven minority stockholders were not happy for long. Ford announced his retirement from the Ford

118

Motor Company and went to California, ostensibly to study nature with his friend John Burroughs, who hated mechanical things and had been seduced by the gift of a Model T.

That automobile, Ford loved to say, changed the old naturalist's life. He began to observe nature from behind a steering wheel. He learned that instead of having to confine himself to a few miles around Slabsides, the whole country was open to him. Out of that automobile grew their friendship.

Although Ford fancied himself as a bird lover, his whole mind was not on the wild life of California. He was preparing a scare for his minority stockholders.

One day he hinted darkly to the reporters who were assigned to keep track of him that he was not through. That was news. Anything he said was news. When reporters in strength came back for more, pressing him to say what he was thinking of, he let it out little by little. Nobody knew yet how really to build an automobile. But if he were to put everything he had learned about it into a new company, starting from scratch, no bankers and no minority stockholders to hinder him, it would certainly be a humdinger. It might well be that nobody had seen anything yet. That was what he was thinking of.

News of this thinking out loud in California caused a panic in the minds of the seven who had just got their big dividends back. If they had thought of selling out privately, now their market was ruined. Who would buy a minority interest in the Ford Motor Company with Ford threatening to become its competitor? If they tried to peddle it in Wall Street, rumors would rise and make matters worse.

But it was a strange thing that men representing unknown principals kept coming around to ask them what they would take for their Ford shares in cash. They named high figures—more than they supposed anybody would pay—and were astonished to find that the anonymous buyer was willing to pay what they asked. One by one they agreed to sell, if the actual money appeared, which it promptly did, without revealing its source—all save Couzens, who wouldn't sell until he knew who the buyer was. He found out. The buyer was Ford. Couzens settled with him personally and got more than anybody else.

There was a sequel, and the high point of it was that a man who held honorary membership in the American Society of Money Cranks performed a feat of financial wizardry that left the bankers begging for air.

To buy out his minority stockholders cost him ninety million dollars. He had to pay them in cash, and he didn't have the money. So he borrowed seventy million from Eastern banks on his notes.

That was his first experience as a borrower. It was a personal matter and did not involve, or at least it ought not to have involved, the Ford Motor Company. However, he did expect to pay off the notes out of its earnings. There he was disappointed. Part of them he did pay out of earnings, but as the latter half of them began to come due business went into a slump. Besides the notes, he owed the government eighteen million dollars on account of income taxes and seven millions more to the employees as their annual bonus. All together he owed fifty-eight millions, and in the company's treasury there was only twenty.

Under the law he could not make a secret of his balance sheet. The facts were there for anybody to see. The Ford Motor Company had to find thirty-eight million dollars in some haste. Where could it get that sum of cash if not from the leering money barons of Wall Street? Their day had come. They would make him forget some of the things he had said about their ways and morals; and Ford on his part thought he could hear them testing their tools of torture.

There were bad rumors that Ford was in trouble. Then he began to suspect that although the rumors came in news dispatches from all over the country, they might perhaps be traced to a single source. This suspicion was confirmed when he learned that "a very fat financial editor was at Battle Creek, sending out bulletins concerning the acuteness of our financial condition."

The very fat financial editor was Clarence W. Barron, owner of a financial news ticker service in Boston and New York and publisher of the *Wall Street Jour-*

nal, who was resting at Battle Creek. He was in fact publishing such bulletins; they were very live news.

Something Ford never told was what took place one morning in his office.

A Wall Street banker appeared—a most agreeable man, optimistic, concealing a bedside manner. He represented himself and others. They understood that owing to an awkward combination of circumstances the Ford Motor Company was in need of a large sum of money. Such things often happened. They understood it perfectly; and they were prepared to provide the money, on one little condition. They would have to insist on naming a treasurer of their own.

Sorensen was present, listening. He saw with his eyes what Ford was thinking. The next ten seconds were memorable in that banker's life. Sorensen said to him: "Dear sir, you may not know it, but you are in danger here. Serious danger. You'd better go while you can. Pardon me, I'll give you a little help."

With that he forcibly propelled the banker out of the room.

6

IN THIS bad dilemma Ford remembered one of his tall maxims. It was that a healthy manufacturing business must be able to create its own capital. When it needed money the shop must produce it. If the shop could not produce it, and you had to go to the bank, then there was something wrong with the shop, and you were

probably already sunk. Borrowing could only post-
pone the day.

So, as he said afterward, he called on the shop, and
the shop "raised a larger sum of money than any bank
in the country could lend."

Owing to the war work that had been going on—war
work being always wasteful—and to the postwar lassi-
tude of labor, and owing somewhat besides to the growing myth of Ford opulence, the shop had got fat. The
first thing was to make it lean again.

The iron ball began to swing. The office force was
cut one half. The other half was not fired; only those
who were unwilling to go back to overalls. The new rule
was: Everybody must produce or get out. To produce
meant to work on the automobile. The Statistical Department was abolished because never yet had statistics
produced an automobile. Three in every five telephones
were torn out because talking about the car did not
build it. Hundreds of blank forms were discontinued; it
took too much time to fill them out. Where there had
been one foreman to every five workers, henceforth
there would be one for every twenty; the unwanted fore-
men could go back to the machines where they came
from. The assembly line went faster. As men began to
be worried about their jobs they were willing to work
harder. The total number of men employed, divided by
the number of cars produced each day, was reduced
from fifteen to nine.

By all of this within the shop, and by a terrific speed-

ing up of transportation outside, the cycle of manufacture—the time from the raw material to the finished
car—was cut from twenty-two to fourteen days. The
overhead, that is, the constant cost above the cost of
manufacture, was reduced from $146 to $93 per car.

So far so good. A lot less money was going out. That,
however, did not solve the problem. A lot more money
had to be coming in.

Suddenly all buying stopped. On hand were large
quantities of raw materials and parts. Out of the stockpiles and out of the bins cars were manufactured at
frantic tempo and as fast as they were made they were
shipped out to Ford dealers all over the country, until
there was nowhere in the whole Ford plant an automobile or the makings of one. The cars were shipped
to the dealers with sight drafts attached, which meant
that the dealers had to pay cash for them on delivery,
whether they wanted them or not. Business was generally bad. Most Ford dealers were already overstocked
and wanted no more cars. That was *their* trouble.

When the stockpiles were gone and the bins were
empty the plant closed down, ostensibly to take inventory; but there was nothing to take inventory of. Then
no money at all was going out. By every mail it came
pouring in.

It worked like this.

In Kansas, Illinois, Texas, anywhere at all, a Ford
dealer would come awake to find that during the night

a certain number of Ford cars had been delivered to him—a carload or a trainload according to the size of his territory—and that was his allotment. Sight drafts attached. Please remit.

The dealer would push his breakfast away and go straight to the bank. To the banker he would say: "I've got to take some more cars. They are out there on the track. Here is the draft and I can't pay it. You will have to lend me the money."

The banker would say: "But you haven't sold the last lot."

The dealer would say: "I know it. I've still got five on the floor and ten in the warehouse. But if I don't take these I'll lose the agency. That's what it means."

The banker would say: "Can you sell them?"

The dealer would say: "I've got to sell them. I think maybe if I put them up at auction I can come out even, and that's all you have to worry about. I'll not make any profit on them."

The banker would be thinking: *I've often loaned this dealer the money to pay his Ford draft. It has always worked out before. He has always been able to sell the cars. This is stiff. But if I refuse him now he'll lose the agency and I'll lose a good customer; and, moreover, if I don't do it the Ford Motor Company will know, and when it makes deposits again in this territory it will pass me by.*

It was a well-known practice of the Ford Motor Com-

125

pany to deposit its surplus funds in a large number of relatively small banks, just to keep them scattered, and every banker wanted to be on its list.

Reluctantly therefore the banker would lend the Ford dealer the money, and the dealer would forget his hat as he propelled himself forth to find some new salesmen, resolved to make two Ford buyers grow where only one grew before.

Once it was done the simplicity of it was absurd. Instead of borrowing the money in Wall Street, Ford obliged thousands of bankers all over the country to lend it to his dealers and the dealers remitted in cash. However, it was doubtful whether any other automobile maker could have done it, even if he had thought of it. The car made it possible. By that time Model T was an economic staple, like cotton or corn; give it time and it would sell itself.

On January 1 the Ford treasury had twenty millions and owed fifty-eight.

On April 1 it had eighty-seven millions, which was enough to pay everything it owed, and twenty-nine millions over.

That was finding it in the shop. Never again did the Ford Motor Company borrow a dollar.

If you say it was a ruthless business, so it was; but Ford would have said that although it was hard on many people, still an insolvent Ford Motor Company or a Ford Motor Company in the hands of Wall Street

The Mechanic and the Wizard:
Unscientific architects of the Ford-Edison World, who
never knew what would work until they tried it. They lived
the same arc . . . heroes of the same mythology. One
played with wheels and the other with an invisible force.
Emotionally they were children. Power was their toy. It
had a built-in volcano. As they set it free in a muscle-weary
world, the roar and heat and light of it filled them with
innocent glee.

When and how the Ford egg was hatched.

The first Ford factory.

The first successful Ford car; not yet the Model T.

Twenty-five years later.
Above: The River Rouge Monster. *Below:* The Experimental Laboratory, all bought and paid for out of profits plowed back.

Two ways of putting the body on.
Above: The Model T at Highland Park. They would try anything once. *Below:* The V-8 at River Rouge. The finished technique.

The first mechanically driven assembly line. It succeeded
one that was pulled by a rope. The rope broke.

A car that came off that assembly line.

Fond Recollections: Twenty years later Ford dragged out of his trinket pile the original racing car in which he made his famous speed record on the ice, reconditioned it and took it out on the Ford Motor Company's proving ground. Just to see if it would still run? No. But to get the feeling of it again. The boy on the running board reproduces the mechanic who rode that way in the race to cut off the gas in case the wide-open throttle should freeze fast. (*See pages 50, 51.*)

The original Model T.

It sold for twenty cents a pound. The number sold was fifteen million. Its life was nineteen years.

Its successor, the Model A.

bankers would have been worse for a great many more. Which would you have?

After that he was entirely free. From where it all started, in the duel with the Dodge brothers, the plant doubled and doubled again, the output doubled and doubled again, but the price of the car never was cut in half. That part never came true, because when he said it he was thinking of Model T, as if it might go on forever. Model T gave way to Model A, and Model A to the V-8.

The earnings went on increasing. A time came when he did not know what to do with them. The business could no longer absorb them. It is forbidden that one tree shall grow to Heaven. When he died he left, besides the Ford empire intact, the largest trust fund in the world. That now is the Ford Foundation, devoted to the welfare of mankind, in ways some of which he would have withered with comment while he lived.

SIX

THE INNOCENT MIND

Wɪᴛʜ his great friend Thomas A. Edison, the self-made wizard, Ford shared a naïve faith in what they called the value of ignorance. *Ignorance* was not the right word. *Innocence* would have been better. What they meant was that in order to act upon a thing in an original manner you have to see it as it is, see it directly, with no labels on it to tell you what it is and no preconceived impressions about it. Thus, as Ford would say, the less you know about a thing beforehand, or think you know, the better.

In the beginning he had no technology. He perhaps could not have defined the word. When it caught up with him he bought it as he would buy a machine, and when he had bought it he controlled it. The use of it was only to find a way to do something he wanted done. His distrust of the expert never softened.

During the Ford Motor Company's offside adventure with aviation I was in Cameron's office one day, talking to a German scientist, when Ford came in. The first

128

thing he said to me was: "Have you seen our aviation plant?"

I said yes, I'd just been looking it over; and then began to twit him gently on the fact that they were developing planes without an air tunnel. He shrugged that off. If they needed an air tunnel they would have one.

On his way out the German scientist whispered in my ear: "You don't understand. Nobody is a scientist here. We are all mechanics."

Ford would drive scientists crazy. He hired enough of them to fill a small asylum; and he understood them much better than they understood him.

His next question to me was to ask if I had any reservations about the future of flying. I acknowledged a few.

"You shouldn't," he said. "You shouldn't. And do you know why you shouldn't?"

"Why?" I asked.

"Because so many young people are putting thought material into it. When you see that you may be sure that something big is coming out of it."

That was more important than a wind tunnel.

I said: "On the ground, before there were any automobiles, you saw streets full of them. Now what do you see in the sky?"

Speaking slowly, looking at the sky through the ceiling, he said: "Many planes. Many, many planes."

129

Just then one of his all-metal planes took off and passed diagonally across the window.

"Animals like that?" I asked.

"Bigger," he said. "Much bigger."

"That's funny," I said. "People think you are going to build little planes for everybody."

"Because I'm a little-car man," he said, "they think I'd be a little-plane man. No. For people, the little car. Not airplanes. They will have to be big. And that reminds me. For a long time I've been seeing an engine in my dreams. It worried me at first because it was where you wouldn't expect a big engine to be, somewhere in space, suspended by sticks and strings. Then it came to me. That's the big engine I want for the big plane I'm talking about."

"How clearly do you see it?" I asked. "Could you draw it?"

"Yes," he said. "I'm drawing it now."

Shortly after that the whole flying machine job went over the back fence. He gave it up on the ground that it was a distraction; he had broken one of his rules to touch it at all. The rule was that everything the Ford Motor Company did should pertain to the manufacture of an automobile.

The engine he had been seeing in his dreams was never built and aviation was left to the young people who were putting thought material into it, until World War II. To the war the most spectacular Ford contribution was the apparitional plant at Willow Run, where

planes for the first time were built in the jaws of canti-
lever bridges.

2

No one could say precisely when Ford the mechanic
became aware of technology as an art. He was always
sensitive to the slur that Model T was not a finely made
car. In early Ford practice there was no fetish of precision. That is why the Model T was noisy and rattled;
that was why also it possessed the animal qualities of
the mountain ass, such as hardihood, extraordinary
powers of endurance, phlegmatic courage and a kind of
cheerfulness when not too much abused. One of Ford's
rich minority stockholders would never ride in it, and
boasted of the fact; and if ever Ford was caught riding
in any other car howls of derisory amusement echoed
in the land.

Once with a party the size of a small caravan he was
driving from New York to Detroit. He was in a fine
English car; behind him was a Packard and behind the
Packard were two Fords. The reporters discovered him
and demanded to know what he was doing in an English
car. Why wasn't he driving a Ford? He said "I'm on
vacation. We are in no hurry. We don't care when we
get home. That's why I'm not in a Ford."

To the aspersion that Model T was a crude utility,
built by the mechanics who scorned precision, he made
one characteristic retort. He would become the American patron of precision. In the arsenal of the Swedish

131

government was a genius named Johansson who had invented block gauges that carried precision of measurement to the millionth part of an inch. That degree of refinement was one hundred times greater than anything the Ford shop could use. Nevertheless, Ford bought the exclusive right to make the gauges, and took Johansson on the payroll, and then so improved the process of manufacture that the supply of gauges was increased and the price reduced, until any machine shop could afford to buy them. "Which proves," he said, "that there is nothing incompatible between *quality* and mass production." With that he went on making Model T's as before. He no more needed a gauge that measured the millionth part of an inch than a blacksmith needs a jeweler's loop.

3

WHETHER Ford got the doctrine of the value of ignorance from Edison, or Edison from him, is an immaterial question. They were born that way. Both made their discoveries by a kind of unspoiled original sense. For their attacks on the impossible they had but one tool. That was trial and error.

Edison was more articulate about it. His mind was more at ease than Ford's in regions of abstraction. He loved to cite examples.

He said to me one day: "Have you seen the New Haven Railroad's electric locomotive?"

I said yes, I had seen it.

"Did you notice how the power was coupled to the wheels?"

I hadn't noticed that particularly.

He said: "The next time you see it you notice that, because I'm going to tell you a story about it."

I did notice it the next time I looked at the New Haven's electric locomotive. Afterward I noticed it in Europe. For some silly reason the problem of getting the power down to the driving wheels of the early electric locomotives had presented awkward difficulties and had been solved in several ways.

The story went on.

"Well," said Edison, "the engineers had that locomotive all finished except for one last thing. They couldn't think of a right way to get the power down to the wheels. They stood around for weeks, looking at it, making little drawings and tearing them up. The boss posted a notice on the bulletin board. A reward for anybody who could make a workable suggestion. Still nothing happened. They were all in a rut. They couldn't see what the problem was. One day the boy from the drafting room stopped at the chief's desk and said, 'I don't know anything about it, but do you think this might work?' He held out a little pencil sketch. The chief said, 'That might work.' They tried it and it did work, and that's what you'll see the next time you look at the locomotive. The point is, that boy was not in a rut."

We got to talking about planes. I happened to say something that caught his attention.

"Good," he said. "Make a little drawing of that and I'll send it along with mine."

"With yours?"

"Yes," he said. "I was in Washington last week. Those Navy aviators came to see me. They said, 'Mr. Edison, we've got the finest plane there is.' I said I was glad to know that. 'Our trouble now,' they said, 'is that we don't know how to go on from here. We've got no new ideas. We were hoping you might give us some.' I said, 'Yes, I'll be glad to.' They all got up and said, 'Come look at the plane.' I told them I was too busy, I just couldn't come. I didn't dare tell them I'd never seen a plane in my life nor if I saw theirs I probably couldn't give them any ideas at all. I told them I'd be thinking about it and when I got home I'd make some drawings and send them down. Here they are." He pulled them out of a pigeonhole.

"Not one of them is worth a damn," he said. "That isn't it. I'll tell you what will happen. They'll say, 'Ah, here are the ideas from Edison.' They will sit down with the drawings and begin to pass them around. After three or four they will begin to make faces. One will say, 'There's nothing here.' Another will say, 'How does he get to be called a great inventor?' Then one will say, 'Will you look at this. See what the idiot has done. He ought to know that won't work, but why didn't he do this?' The instant one says, 'Why didn't he do this?,' they've got an idea of their own. They are on their way again. That's all these drawings are good for."

I was in Edison's laboratory one day when they were playing with a rock that contained a valuable substance and hated to give it up. The rock was in a big wooden tank, immersed, and they were experimenting with a catalytic chemical that would leach the valuable substance out and release it, only it took too long and because it was slow it was too costly. Tacked to the tank was a chart on which the chemists kept a record of the reaction time. Once every day Edison came in, looked at the chart and grunted, because the reaction time line kept running flat—no improvement at all. One day he said: "Put in more of that stuff." The chief chemist said: "We can't go any further that way, Mr. Edison. We've already put it in to the saturation point. Any more will be inert." Edison said: "Put in five times as much," and went away. The chemists looked at each other, thinking: "That's what he knows about chemistry. Well, he's the boss." They put in five times as much, and then for a reason no chemist could give the time line began to rise.

4

So they worked—the innocents, who did many things that were impossible because they didn't know any better. They didn't mind failure. "One who fears failure," said Ford, "limits his activities. Failure is only the opportunity more intelligently to begin again."

When Ford was playing with one of his most exciting toys—the Detroit, Toledo & Ironton Railroad—he watched the track writhe as a train went over it and thought how unmechanical it was to lay steel rails on wooden ties buried in a bed of cinders. Why not a rigid roadway, with rails laid in concrete? The old railroad men told him it wouldn't work; with that kind of roadway the train would jump off at the first curve. He wouldn't believe it, and had a stretch of experimental track built the way he wanted it. Then he watched a train jump off at the curve, and said, "Do it again." It jumped off again. He had them do it a third time. Then he said: "Tear it up."

Ford, Edison, Harvey Firestone and John Burroughs used to go camping together, for recreation they thought, but really for the pleasures of adversative communion, until, as it would be, such a caravan of Olympians began to be trailed by reporters. That spoiled it.

Edison told me this. One evening at the campfire Ford began to tell of the tractor he was building. The design was all complete but for the steering mechanism. He had not been able to get that right. He explained what the requirements were. It had to be powerful, sensitive, quick, and so on. "Think about it," he said to Edison. When he had thought about it Edison made a little drawing. Ford glanced at it and said it wouldn't do. Then he made a drawing and showed it to Edison, who said he was sure that wouldn't work, and Ford agreed with him. They swapped several drawings that way, and then Ford said, "Here's one I think will

136

work." Edison looked at it and said: "That's the worst one yet." Ford said, "No; I think that will work." "And," said Edison, "that's the one he tried and that's the one that worked."

Fumbling they understood.

As the fumbling mind may arrive at truth, so the fumbling hand may make a precision tool, or a tool that will unerringly describe a straight line—a thing the hand itself cannot do and a thing, moreover, that has first to exist in the imagination because it is nonexistent in nature. Fumblers they were, purposeful, persistent and sometimes lucky. Or you may think of them as anglers blindfold, casting their hooks into the mouth of the void, hoping to draw Leviathan forth. When they were wrong it was like losing a fish they had never seen, and one that maybe was never there. They often were wrong.

A time came when the Ford Motor Company decided to electrify itself. The engineers went forth to look, and when they had seen how everybody else did it they came back to design an installation the Ford way. The one thing they added was very high voltage, higher than anybody had used before. When they were all ready to turn it on, Ford said: "Now wait a minute. We don't know much about electricity. Mr. Edison does. He knows everything about it. I'd like to have him look this over." So Edison came, looked it over and went home. Ford called his engineers in and faced them uneasily. "Mr. Edison has got me worried," he said.

"He likes what we've done. He thinks it's a fine job. But he says it's dangerous. He's made me afraid of it."

One of the engineers said: "When he says it's dangerous, what does he mean?"

"Dangerous," said Ford. "You know what that means. Dangerous."

"He means it might kill somebody?" the engineer persisted.

"Certainly," said Ford. "That's what dangerous means."

The engineer said: "Well, Mr. Ford, if you are going to get killed by electricity does it make any difference to you whether it's one thousand volts or ten thousand?"

For a moment Ford stared thoughtfully at the engineer. Then he said: "Ah! That fool Edison. Turn it on."

5

FOR all their agreement on the doctrine of original perception, which they called the value of ignorance, these two minds differed remarkably in their separate ways of working. Ford was hand-minded. If you had cut off his hands you would have crippled his mind. As for Edison, the loss of his hands probably would not have affected his mind at all. He had no brains in his hands. The contrast was noticeable when they walked among moving machines. Ford could not look at a machine without feeling it in his tissues, sympathetically, and

138

if he touched one it was as if he touched a living thing. Edison was distant with machines and if he touched one he did it timidly, as if it might do an unexpected thing or snap at him.

Ford's way was to let his mind run free, like a puckish servant; it made many unnecessary and willful excursions, and yet did generally come back with what it was sent to bring.

Edison bridled his mind and made it answerable to his will. He had a curious way of watching it work. He once told me about inventing the way to make four simultaneous messages go by one wire without mixing.

"You start with one," he said, "that's fast here." (Between the thumb and forefinger.) "Then you reach out there for two, which isn't so far, and you get it to where you can hold it tight along with one. Then three. That's away out there. You find it and bring it in slowly and then, just as you think you've got it, away it goes, and two with it. So you bring two back and reach again for three. After a while you get three in place. Then four. Four is away, away out there, and just as you are about to get hold of it, three flies off again."

And so it went on and on until at last, when he had four in place and could hold it fast, his right arm was trembling from the strain and great beads of perspiration were standing out on his forehead. Merely from the recollection of it.

Ford, if he had happened to want the same thing, would have suspended an interrogation mark in the top

139

of his head; then he would have gone about using his hands, tinkering with tools, whittling maybe, or talking by the hour on things he was not thinking about—all the time expecting the answer to come. And it might come.

He apparently never got anything out of books. "I don't like to read books," he said. "They muss up my mind." And again: "Machines are to a mechanic what books are to a writer."

Edison worked, lived and slept with books. His library was a part of his equipment, like a bench tool. Not a general library. It was a record of his mental journeys. Each subject he had ever explored had its shelf or two of books, some of them as forgotten as travel folders, and yet never discarded. Rubber, chemistry, botany, metallurgy, physics, sound, rare substances, geology, economics.

The economics shelf was sad and dusty. One night by the campfire Ford asked him to put his mind on money and invent a whole new monetary system, simple, scientific and banker-proof, for the people. The idea was not entirely absurd. Simon Newcomb, a great American astronomer, once out of sheer exasperation turned his mind to political economy and produced the finest, clearest textbook in the language. But Edison's mind was not like that.

The first thing he did was to get someone to make him a list of economic titles. He read them all and then produced his plan. His Wall Street friends went over

140

it respectfully and said: "We are sorry to tell you, Mr. Edison, there's nothing in it." Edison said: "There's got to be something in it. I've spent three months on it."

He took it then to the financial editor of the New York *Times*, old Sandy Noyes, who said the same thing. Adolph Ochs, the publisher, said anyhow a monetary system invented by Edison had popular news value, if nothing else, and gave it full publicity. There was nothing in it, really. What Edison could not understand was that people's trouble with money comes from nothing money does to them but from what they do to money. Almost any monetary system would work if you could leave people out, as he did.

6

Never himself a profit maker, Edison envied that side of Ford. It dazzled him.

Ford envied the qualities of Edison's mind, without ever being able to say precisely what they were—natural powers of abstraction, analysis and synthesis, consciously if rudely exercised. He called Edison "the world's greatest scientist," whereas Edison was no more a scientist than Ford was and disliked to be named one. To that dubious eulogy Ford added: "I'm not sure that he isn't also the world's worst businessman. He knows almost nothing about business."

The friendship between them was famous. On Edison's side it was whimsical, indulgent and Socratic; and on Ford's side it was romantic and a little extravagant.

They lived the same arc, one overtaking the other. They were the copybook prodigies of their time, heroes of the same mythology, and not rivals. In the Detroit Institute of Arts there is a mural by Diego Rivera in which you may find them both as a composite symbol of machine man.

Power was their plaything. As they unchained and set it free in a muscle-weary world, the roar and light and heat of it filled them with innocent glee. When Archimedes said, "Give me whereon to rest my fulcrum and I will move the world," he was boasting of a new toy which we call the principle of the lever. Their toy had a built-in volcano.

Emotionally they were children.

Once when Edison was invited to Greenfield Village, where Ford had embalmed American life as it was before Model T, he found there what he took at first to be a replica of the old frame shop in which he had done some of his great work. It was not a replica. It was the shop itself. Ford had sent out men to recover the very boards wherever they might be, and the lumber that was in the wizard's bench, and to dig in his forgotten dump for objects that might be restored, such as a broken mortar and pestle that could be mended—and here it all was, just as he remembered it, so cunningly re-created that he could believe he had never left it and that everything that had happened in the years since he moved out of it had been only imagined. As he touched

142

the familiar objects he said, "I could sit down here and go right to work with my old tools" and began to weep.

7

WONDERFUL they may be, and yet the values of ignorance are not without price. When men say anything is possible if you don't know any better, they express a kind of contempt for history, experience and expert opinion. It is a shibboleth and may be very exciting; but it has almost no other merit. When men begin to believe it, as if it were true, they are bound to go on to the thought that if anything is possible, so anything may be true, with the cynical notation that what people generally believe is probably wrong. With that, they expose themselves to every cracked wind that blows. They imagine themselves to be skeptics whereas in fact they are gullibles. A skeptic doubts everything. These willful innocents, however, doubt what is commonly believed because it *is* commonly believed, and then in place of it they believe something else because it is contrary.

In his own mechanical world Ford could not be fooled. A thing worked or it didn't work, and that was finality. Outside of that world he was a very credulous man. Let it be a metaphysical thing, a property of the ethos, a political matter involving passion and prejudice—let it be anything the truth of which you can neither prove nor disprove with a monkey wrench or on the work bench, and there in every case he preferred the perverse opinion. If there was no perverse opinion, so much the better; he made one up.

What he could believe without cracking the pot was evidence of a kind of fool-proof sanity. He was aware of himself in that aspect.

He did not mind being thought a fool. It was not bad to be a fool for what one believed was right. Then, not to leave himself or the fool entirely in the lurch, he would add: "The best part of it is that fools sometimes live to prove they were right."

At that moment he was probably thinking of the Ford Peace Ship, which made him the fool of the world. That was the weirdest single episode of his life.

World War I was going into its second year. The Americans had not yet got into it. One day a woman pacifist in cotton stockings from Budapest crashed Ford's office to tell him that the combatant nations all wanted to stop, only they didn't know how; in the chancelleries of Europe, on both sides, they were praying for someone to come and show them how. He believed it. She told him that as a man to whom anything was possible he could do it. He believed he could. He believed he could stop the war with, first, a Ford sermon such as he could inspire his publicity people to write, and then by leading a shipful of pacifists to Europe under the slogan "Get the boys out of the trenches by Christmas."

144

The newspapers yelled, Whoopee! For the reporters it was a savage feast of whale meat. The American government was embarrassed and treated it all very coldly. European governments asked sternly if this American fantast thought he was going to start a soldiers' strike. That would be sinister. Ford had been quoted as saying that it would be—a world-wide strike against war. This he repudiated. It was nothing like that. The idea was that all people alike, statesmen, generals and soldiers, wanted to stop fighting. What they lacked was a Ford formula. He said: "I don't care what the critics say, I have believed other things possible, and they were."

The Rev. Samuel S. Marquis, Ford's pastor, went along in the role of Sancho Panza. Writing of it afterward, he told how he wrestled with his unmanageable knight on the eve of the ship's departure. Ford kept saying: "It is right to try to stop war, isn't it?" To that the pastor would only say yes. Then Ford would say: "Don't you believe that what is right is bound to succeed?" The argument that there was a right way with right things and that a right thing attempted the wrong way might fail moved him not at all.

But Cervantes' Don Quixote was not the world's richest automobile manufacturer. This one was. He was sick and cold and hurting with disillusionment when the Peace Ship arrived in Scandinavia, and permitted himself to be whisked away from his quarreling pacifists, by his bodyguard, and to be put aboard the next

145

ship home, very glad perhaps that his owlish friend Edison had refused to go along.

He never talked much about it afterward. He had trusted the information that some of the nations were anxious for peace and would welcome his demonstration. In the hope that this was true he had financed the expedition to Stockholm in what had since been called the Peace Ship. He did not regret the attempt. That it failed had not convinced him that it was not worth trying. He was one to learn more from failure than from success. What he had learned on that trip was worth the time and the money, and as to whether his information was true or false, he did not care.

8

HE BELIEVED that war was "a purely manufactured evil"—manufactured by international bankers, munitions makers and profiteers, who had perfected a "definite technique" of wickedly exciting nations to hate and fear one another.

He believed there existed in the world a secret cabal of super-Machiavellian men, acting upon every government, every great business organization and every agency of publicity, with intent to create panics, depressions and states of political frenzy; riding the aftermath of dire events, like masked ghouls, they extended their power and made off with the spoils.

He believed there was a Jewish conspiracy to corrupt and destroy the Christian world.

He believed the Protocols of Zion.

For seven years he carried on a campaign of defamation against the Jews. For its spirit of enterprise, for marvel of invention and for valor of ignorance, it had no parallel in all the literature of anti-Semitism. He did not write it. Cameron, his editor, did the writing, as everybody knew. The organ was the Dearborn *Independent*, Ford's private magazine, which seven thousand Ford dealers, Jewish and non-Jewish, were obliged to buy and promote. The first series of articles in the *Independent* began: "There is a race a part of humanity which has never yet been received as a welcome part." The articles were reprinted in four books and widely distributed, not for profit.

The curious fact was that Ford probably believed himself when he said he was not anti-Semitic. He was only trying once for all to settle the immemorial Jewish question. How? By obliging Jews to see themselves as he saw them; and he expected good Jews to stand with him. One of his good Jews was a rabbi in Detroit to whom he presented each year a Ford car in token of friendship. He was astonished and hurt when one year the rabbi refused to accept his gift, and called him on the telephone to ask what was wrong. Had something come between them?

Then suddenly he recanted the whole of it in a statement that was abject and absurd. He blamed his subordinates. He had been too busy to notice what they were doing in his name, until certain trustworthy

147

friends informed him that Jews everywhere were terribly resentful and regarded him as their enemy. "This," he said, "led me to direct my personal attention to this subject in order to ascertain the exact nature of these articles. As a result of this survey I confess I am deeply mortified that this journal, which is intended to be constructive and not destructive, has been made the medium for resurrecting exploded fictions, for giving currency to the so-called protocols of the wise men of Zion, which have been demonstrated, as I learn, to be gross forgeries, and for contending that the Jews have been engaged in a conspiracy to control the capital and the industries of the world, besides laying at their door many offenses against decency, public order and good morals. Had I appreciated even the general nature, to say nothing of the details, of these utterances, I would have forbidden their circulation without a moment's hesitation."

Cameron could not have written a thing so lame. Nor did Ford write it; he only signed it. To believe it you would have to suppose not only that he had never read what his own magazine was saying but that for seven years he had been deaf, since his dealers and his associates had been telling him all the time that his campaign was hurting the sale of Ford cars.

The Dearborn *Independent* went to the ash can, to the great relief of Ford dealers; Cameron accepted the scapegoat's burden and lived it out. All the rest of it the shop absorbed. Model A was just then coming out.

There was a last word. It appeared in the chapter entitled "Things in General," of *My Life and Work*, by Henry Ford, published in 1922. Ford could not have written it. The style is Cameron's. However, since it was Ford's autobiography and since he must have approved it, it was he who said—

"The work which we describe as Studies in the Jewish Question, and which is variously described by antagonists as 'the Jewish campaign,' 'the attack on the Jews,' the 'anti-semitic program,' and so forth, needs no explanation to those who have followed it. . . . There had been observed in this country certain streams of influence which were causing a marked deterioration in our literature, amusements, and social conduct; business was departing from its old time substantial soundness; a general letting down of standards was felt everywhere. It was not the robust coarseness of the white man, the rude indelicacy of, say, Shakespeare's characters, but a nasty Orientalism which has insidiously affected every channel of expression—and to such an extent that it was time to challenge it. The fact that these influences are all traceable to one racial source is a fact to be reckoned with, not only by us but by the intelligent people of the race in question. Our work does not pretend to say the last word on the Jew in America. It says only the word which describes his obvious present impress on the country. When that impress is changed the report of it can be changed. For the present, then, the question is wholly in the Jews' hands. If they are as wise as they claim to be, they will labor to make Jews American instead of laboring to make America Jewish. The genius of the United States of America is Christian in the broadest sense, and its density is to remain American. . . . The work was taken up without personal motives. When it reached a stage where we believed the American people could grasp the key, we let it rest for the time. Our enemies say that we began it for revenge and that we laid it down in fear. Time will show that our critics are merely dealing in evasion because they dare not tackle the main question. Time will also show that we are better friends to the Jews' best interests than are those who praise them to their faces and criticize them behind their backs." *

9

ANOTHER debit against the value of ignorance may be noted. You may see a thing clearly, but the more clearly you see it the more probable it is that you will see it in isolation, with no relation to anything else. Two or more different things may be as one in principle. If you see them separately and act upon them separately you will probably find yourself involved in contradictions, that is, contradictions in principle. This will be true of things that cannot be taken apart on the bench.

Thus Ford.

* *My Life and Work,* by Henry Ford. Copyright 1922 by Doubleday & Co., Inc.

He thought the railroads were very badly managed and was in a continuous feud with them for the way they handled his freight and what they charged for doing it. Therefore it was not surprising that while supporting President Wilson for re-election he was for government ownership and operation of the railroads. Yet when he got a railroad of his own he hotly resented government regulations.

And the same again with public utilities. He was publicly on record as an advocate of government ownership, yet when it came to the water power development at Muscle Shoals on the Tennessee River—an unfinished government project from World War I—which he tried very hard to buy, he stipulated in his offer of purchase that the government should not touch him for one hundred years.

Looking at government, he could say that when you got a whole country thinking that Washington was a sort of Heaven and that behind its clouds dwelt omniscience and omnipotence, you were educating that country into a dependent state of mind which augured ill for the future. The government was servant. The moment the people became adjuncts of government, then the law of retribution began to work, for such a relation was unnatural, immoral and inhuman.

Then a time came when he looked at the presidency, himself in the White House, and that was very different. He signed an article in *Collier's* entitled "If I Were President," and nobody who read it could doubt that

Henry Ford as Mr. President would put plenty of omnipotence into government, if not omniscience. He suggested that it might be necessary for industry sometime
to absorb government, which meant of course that in
that case government would be run like the Ford Motor
Company.

What was perhaps the wildest contradiction in him
was the one least observed.

For the public that bought the Ford car he had a
very deep respect. He was grateful for its long loyalty
and felt an obligation to satisfy its expectations. It was
always right, it was sovereign; even when it bought
fewer and fewer Model T's it was still right, and he
made a new and better car, more to its liking.

But for the public as people he had a lively contempt. He cared nothing for people's opinions, which
he thought were generally wrong; all the more people
cared for his, and clamored for them. Reporters were
assigned to dog him. To avoid them he sometimes went
in and out through the windows. Yet he liked it, too.
If he said church was good for those who needed it, that
carrots were the perfect food, that poverty was a
crime, or that the League of Nations would save the
world from the international bankers, it was news. He
got the habit of sounding off and loved the newspaper
headlines. He could hardly have failed to get the notion that any thought that popped into his head was
worth printing. It probably never occurred to him to
wonder why. Any reporter could have told him.

Distrust of the expert is a native American prejudice. Any man may do anything. Are we not founded on
the faith that the obscure boy may become president,
and one not much worse than another? Greatness is a
Jack-of-all-trades. The irrational assumption follows
that a man who has achieved greatly in one thing will
have important opinions to impart on many things.
This is the theory of the value of ignorance turned
around and coming back. Maybe Ford did it to himself;
maybe the people whose opinions he despised did it to
him.

Touching anything that was Caesar's he was consist-
ently adamant. From this you may deduce that many of
his extravagant sayings were shockers only.

Through all of his career the conservative grimsires
of the American free enterprise system regarded him
with alarm; he was a dangerous maverick, almost a
revolutionary, at the least a menace, an anticapitalist
capitalist—certainly the last man you could trust to
defend the premises with his life. And yet, when the New
Deal came, he was the one who had the will and the courage to stand against it, *and he stood alone*.

But for the Ford Motor Company, it would have to
be written that the surrender of American business to
government was unanimous, complete and uncondi-
tional. Its representatives went to Washington in relays
and signed Blue Eagle codes, binding themselves under
pain of fine and imprisonment, not to compete any
more, not to cut prices, to limit production, and not to

153

increase their capacity for producing wealth without a certificate of sanction. All of Ford's competitors in the motor industry signed. He refused. The White House sent for him. When he came back and was asked what had happened he said the President had talked a good deal about the Roosevelt ancestry. "Old Iron Pants" Hugh Johnson, boss of the Blue Eagle, threatened him with extinction, but in vain. Ford said the Blue Eagle was not the law, which it was, and that Hugh Johnson's word wasn't law, although for everybody else it was. Public opinion was against him because people had been persuaded that competition and price cutting prevented recovery from the Great Depression. That left him cold. His associates were scared and told him it might ruin the Ford Motor Company. He stopped his ears. He never did sign. His vindication was that the United States Supreme Court at length declared the law unconstitutional and killed the Blue Eagle.

In moments of social exuberance he had advocated higher income and inheritance taxes. In the end he beat the tax collector by leaving his surplus wealth to the Ford Foundation for the good of mankind, which is not taxable.

SEVEN

IN THE GLARE

Keepers of the grand tradition treated Ford's role in politics as that of Bottom in *Midsummer Night's Dream,* wearing the head of an ass, only that Bottom knew it and Ford didn't. Still, no one could be really sure. Maybe Ford did know it. He might have been president. If it was a spell it broke suddenly, and he saved himself by turning his back on the whole business, with no word of explanation, to the dismay of an idolatrous retinue and a great following that was anxious to get itself counted in favor of standing government on its ancient head.

It began when President Wilson asked him to stand in Michigan for the United States Senate. Mr. Wilson was a Democrat and Ford was a Republican, but only, as he said, for the same reason that he had ears, namely, that he was born that way. He was for the League of Nations, and that was why the President wanted him in the Senate.

He expected to be nominated by both parties. The Republican party refused to have him, which obliged

155

him to accept nomination on the Democratic ticket. His opponent was Truman H. Newberry, who belonged to Detroit's aristocratic clan and had been in Theodore Roosevelt's cabinet.

A political machine was something that Ford knew nothing about, and for once his theory of the value of ignorance betrayed him. He made no campaign at all. Yet he was so sure of victory that he celebrated it with a dinner of the innocents before the votes were counted.

He was beaten. This made him very bitter, because he believed the Republicans had bought the result, which was apparently true. Besides making a great outcry about it, blaming his defeat on the league of wickedness in Wall Street, he turned out what he called his gang to explore the crime. It produced a great mass of damaging evidence, on which Newberry was indicted, tried and found guilty of spending more money than the law allowed. It was a celebrated case. A man who was to be in years to come successively Justice of the United States Supreme Court, Republican candidate for president against Wilson and then Secretary of State, Charles Evans Hughes, took Newberry's case to the Supreme Court, on the ground that the law under which he had been found guilty was unconstitutional, and won. A Democratic Senate refused to unseat Newberry after that; but when the Republicans got control of the Senate in the next election and threatened to reopen the case, he called it enough and icily resigned.

156

2

THE habits of political bees are not too well known. We observe only the reactions of those who get stung. How, for example, did the presidential bee know that the time to sting Ford was when, with his exulting friends, he was celebrating his election to the United States Senate before the votes were counted? You might think any rational bee would have known better; would have waited at least until the sting of the senatorial bee had worn off. But this bee was right. It was at that dinner, so far as anybody can remember, that Ford for president was for the first time seriously proposed, in a toast by Harvey Firestone, who said he would give half his fortune to see it. True, the Michigan delegation to the Republican National Convention in 1916 had mentioned his name, and so had the Nebraska delegation, but nobody had thought this to be more than gesturing; even Ford passed it off lightly when reporters asked him, not too gravely, what he had to say.

He said he supposed running a government was like running a factory, or that it ought to be if it wasn't.

But now there was no mistaking the omens that appeared in the Ford firmament nor the direction of the winds that moved on the waters beneath. Ford-for-President Clubs took a definite form. The first one at Dearborn was seed for one hundred and fifty all over

157

the country. The seven thousand Ford dealers began to get campaign material.

In the Dearborn *Independent* Cameron wrote: "The next President of the United States will be a man who can read a blueprint and who understands the problems of production and how to keep men employed."

To all who went to and fro it was evident that the mind of the Ford Motor Company had turned its surplus energy to the exciting business of amateur president making. Topside executives began to dream of cabinet titles, such as Mr. Secretary this and Mr. Secretary that, and pinned them to one another playfully. Allan L. Benson, who did a book entitled *The New Henry Ford*, tells that at a lunch one day Ford pointed to one of his staff and said, "That's the kind of man I would appoint Secretary of the Navy." Benson was then doing a series of articles on what people might expect if Ford were president.

Arthur Brisbane began to appear, with welcome on the door mat. Brisbane was a prodigious journalist who simplified knowledge for the masses and lived in Hearst's most expensive cage. He could see a bandwagon before it came round the bend and carried his ladder with him. He saw some that were not there. This one was there all right, the same clumsy old-fashioned vehicle it had always been, and that was what was strange about it, seeing whose bandwagon it was. Brisbane told Ford that Hearst was coming out for him, and Hearst did, predicting that Ford could have the

158

country on a third ticket if neither of the old parties wanted him. The popular magazines began to take straw ballots and Ford's name ran very high.

The few friends who kept their feet on the stolid earth received gay farewells. Edison's want of enthusiasm was personal. It might not be bad for the country, or he didn't care, but for Ford, he thought, it would be terrible. He said to Ford, "Why, you can't even make a speech." Well, he couldn't. On the one occasion when he had been persuaded to look an audience in the face he behaved as you do in the dream of appearing in the public square on a holiday without your trousers. Toward documents of all kinds and long papers he felt a positive aversion, as all of his associates knew. His old partner, Jim Couzens, now a United States Senator, said publicly in Detroit that if Ford were ever elected president he would learn the meaning of the word "humiliation."

By this time the enigma that was the Ford mind had become a matter of national concern. What was it like —not according to the myth, but in fact? Thoughtful people wanted to know. He was studied from the point of view of a psychiatrist, from that of a social reformer, from that of a political realist, and so on, and when their reports were all in the man everybody knew was a riddle still. Norman Hapgood said it was the mind of a child full of wheels. That was true. But what of it? What Hapgood did not know, or could not have explained if he had thought of it, was that for years, in

159

the merciless struggle for advantage, that same mind had baffled the very best brains in the freest, the most competitive and the most imaginative industry ever created until then by human intelligence.

It happened one day in the Detroit Club that three members of the famous Ford alumni, men who had worked with him through stress and frenzy, sat for several hours exchanging recollections of him. One was William S. Knudsen, who had been his production manager before Sorensen and who was, next to Sorensen, perhaps the best production man in the world. They had no reason to love him. All three of them had been thought indispensable; all three had gone down the same spillway, pushed from behind. Yet they bore him no animosity.

At last one of them said slowly: "Bill, how d-i-d h-e d-o i-t?"

They all knew what *it* meant. A pronoun for something that has no name, no shape, no reason to be, and nevertheless acts. It was the kind of thing Ford did from which afterward you deduced the existence of an nth faculty, a mysterious gadget that worked without ticking, and produced the unexpected answer.

Knudsen said: "Even in little things. Say we are going to buy a certain part for the automobile instead of making it for ourselves, maybe the distributor head, an assembled part made up of many pieces. The samples come in. The production men, the engineers and the

160

technicians spend days going over them, taking them apart, testing one against another, making notes and tying labels to them. Then they are all spread out on a table, maybe thirty of them, ready for Ford. He comes in, looks at them for two or three minutes with his squinted eyes, says, 'That one,' and walks out. It's that one, sure enough. But how does he do it?"

Another said: "Or suppose Ford and the three of us are standing on the corner downstairs. There is a silly bet. Who can get to the opposite corner of the block first without running? There are only three ways—two ways around the block and one way through a building. We start, each taking one of the three ways, and Ford disappears. The three of us get there all at about the same time, but there is Ford already, gazing up at the cornice of a building as if he wondered what a cornice was for. How did he get there? You tell me. My guess is he wouldn't know himself how he did it."

That satisfied them as perfect allegory. There was nothing more to say. Thus three old hardheads who had been his shopmates, who knew his ways, his astonishing vagaries, his whimsical and sometimes puerile contradictions, could reduce themselves to a state of bemused silence by asking themselves how a child mind full of wheels could so often arrive first at the opposite corner.

What good was their testimony?

Oswald Garrison Villard, who was a leader of liberal thought in his time, wrote that in many years of politi-

cal observation he had never known a candidate so un-
fit; if Ford got to the White House anything might
happen.

Arthur Vandenberg, who was later a member of the
United States Senate, bricklayer on the United Nations
job and Republican leader of the country's bipartisan
foreign policy, was then editor of the Grand Rapids
Herald. He fairly set the key for the conservative press
when he wrote that no other citizen whom you might
suppose to be responsible had to his discredit so many
erratic interviews on public questions, so many dubious
opinions, such bland ignorance of American history and
American experience, in brief, so much political nonsense.

That could be true. As Cameron said, the Ford mind
was a ceaseless mill that produced an enormous quantity of chaff; yet if you screened the chaff you would
find something like this:

"Two things men grow tired of—meaningless poverty and meaningless prosperity. Something else has to
be added. The fact is that both poverty and plutocracy
are insufferably dull."

However, none of this made the slightest bit of difference to the people who wanted to vote for Ford.
They wanted to vote for him all the more. Adhering to
him were such diverse elements of the citizenry as perhaps could not have united before or since on one candidate.

Labor had not yet turned against him. He was still

the man who stood on the side of the worker against the selfish employer.

Farmers were for him. Had he not brought the automobile to the farm?

Pacifists were for him, remembering the Peace Ship.

There was still a pro-German element, hanging over from World War I, and that was for him.

All who hated Wall Street, the international banker and something they called the money trust, would vote for him.

The prohibitionists he had in his pocket.

Radicals and anticapitalists to whom the profit motive was anathema forgot that he was not only the greatest profit maker of his age but one of the few who had ever pushed the logic of free, competitive capitalism to its extreme conclusion; they seemed not to understand, or to care, why he denounced the profit motive; it was enough that he did it and he was their witness.

It was a curious fact that almost nobody ever thought of Ford as a rich man. He conformed to no popular image of what a rich man was. He was not money-rich. His wealth was in things. He abhorred idle things, idle money and idle people; and he produced so much more wealth than he consumed that what he consumed was as nothing.

All the soft-money ballots of the West would fall in his pile, because he had said the gold standard was a device invented by bankers to oppress the people and

163

was at heart a greenbacker. Even his anti-Jewish crusade was not a pure liability. It was likely to make votes for him in the South and Middle West.

Lastly, millions of Ford car owners transferred to him the kind of bellicose affection they felt for Model T. Fanciful as that may sound, it was important. Model T was the little man's car. First and last, Ford was the little man's man.

Altogether, he was a very dangerous candidate.

Coolidge was then President, in place of Harding, who had died, and was the natural Republican candidate for the next campaign. Ford was his only formidable rival, as a Republican, as a Democrat or on a third ticket.

3

WHETHER Ford really wanted to be president, or how much, which was always debatable, there was one thing he had set his heart on. That was Muscle Shoals, the name of a thing now almost forgotten. During World War I the government started an immense hydroelectric power development on the Tennessee River at a place called Muscle Shoals, with intent to make atmospheric nitrate for explosives. Before it was completed the war to end war was won, and since there was not going to be any more war there was no further need for nitrate, except for fertilizer, and unless the government was going to go into the fertilizer business, which it wasn't, or into the electric power business,

which at that time it did not intend doing, the problem
was what to do with the unfinished works at Muscle
Shoals.

Ford had got from Edison a romantic notion of the
possibilities of hydroelectric power. He had already
been building little dams on the upreaches of the River
Rouge and hitching small factories to them, hoping to
create idyllic industrial villages around the native farm
life. Either out of his own head or out of Edison's came
a prevision of what we now know as TVA—that is, the
Tennessee Valley Authority, which was created during
the Roosevelt administration in a spirit of social adventure. It has transformed the Tennessee Valley region,
chained down its floods, covered it with electric light
and power, and made over the lives of the people, as a
demonstration of planned welfare under the hand of
government.

What Ford might have done with it in place of what
the government did might have been very different. No
comparison is possible, however, because his plans were
vague. It was something big enough to play with; it
would be developed in the Ford way, service before
profit—and leave the rest of it to him. That was all he
would say. But he wanted it very badly. When he offered to buy it from the government, at a white elephant
price, public opinion immediately divided. A great
many people, perhaps a large majority at that time,
were for letting Ford have it, if not quite on his own
terms, then on any reasonable basis. On the other side

stood an aggressive and extremely obdurate minority, led by Senator Norris, who afterward became the father of TVA. These minority people not only quarreled with the Ford terms; their political creed endeared them to public works and made them hostile to any private development of water power.

As the controversy developed the country was entertained with fantastic previews of what Ford would do with Muscle Shoals. At the very least, he would make fertilizer as cheap as dirt and bust the fertilizer trust. If that was not enough for the farmers, then, as he had brought the automobile to the farm, so he would bring hydroelectric power to all rural life. There was a silly land boom in the Tennessee Valley. Ford town sites were laid out and lots were peddled in the North. In Congress at the same time Senator Norris and his cult were calling the Ford offer the swindle of the age.

What with the Muscle Shoals kettle coming to an angry boil and the Ford bandwagon building seats higher and higher to accommodate more passengers, there was gaiety in the nation such as no later children would ever know. Something was going to happen.

Then one day President Coolidge asked Henry Ford to come to the White House. That gave the bandwagon a lurch and made a holiday for the political cynics, who said all with one voice: "It's a trade. There is going to be a trade. Ford's candidacy for Muscle Shoals. That sly Calvin Coolidge!" That possibility may still be mentioned in political histories.

But there was no trade. Coolidge could not have bargained to deliver Muscle Shoals to anybody. Only Congress could do that. Ford on his part was not a man to trade away his heart's desire. It was nevertheless a strange episode.

As Ford was setting out for Washington he happened to run into Roy D. McClure and took him along for company. McClure was his doctor, his companion on many sudden excursions, and head of the Henry Ford Hospital. When they got to Washington, McClure held back. Ford said: "Come on, come on. Maybe you will learn something." McClure therefore was present through the entire interview and long afterward he told me about it.

The President and Ford exchanged compliments and talked pleasantly on matters of commonplace interest great and small—the harvest, the farmer's dollar, the war debts, the state of Europe, the December weather. Ford did most of the talking, as anyone who knew Coolidge might suppose. Two subjects were never mentioned. One was politics. The other was Muscle Shoals. It was not a long visit.

On their way back to the railroad station, Ford said to McClure: "There's a man who means all right."

At Baltimore the reporters caught Ford and overwhelmed him. What about Muscle Shoals?

"Muscle Shoals?" he said. "Where is Muscle Shoals?"

They knew it was somewhere in the Tennessee River Valley.

"Where does the Tennessee River begin?" Ford asked.

Nobody knew that.

"Muscle Shoals," he repeated, as if it were a curious thing. "How do you spell it. Is it m-u-s-s-e-l, something that people eat, or m-u-s-c-l-e, like something in your arm?"

When they stuttered on that one he said: "See. What's the use of discussing a thing you know so little about?"

And that was all they could get out of him.

A few days later he calmly announced that he was not a candidate. The country was safe with Coolidge. He would not think of running against him.

President Coolidge did recommend to Congress that the Muscle Shoals property be sold to private interests for private development. He almost certainly would have done that in any case, for he believed very strongly that the government ought not to compete with private business, in power, in fertilizer, or anything else. Ford never did get it. Coolidge was elected, and after him came Hoover, yet Congress did not act. In the end the New Deal got Muscle Shoals.

In three volumes of homily and autobiography written with Samuel Crowther in 1922, 1926 and 1930, Ford's struggles with the Satan of politics are missing. They were not so important after all. On Muscle Shoals he authorized a statement in 1926, saying:

"More than two years ago we made the best bid we

knew how to make. No definite action has been taken on
it. A simple affair of business which should have been
decided by anyone within a week has become a compli-
cated political affair. We are not in politics and we are
in business. We do not intend to be drawn into politics.

"We have been and still are deeply interested in
Muscle Shoals as a national asset. That concerns every
one of us as citizens. I have two main principles with
regard to Muscle Shoals. First, it should be operated
as a combined industrial unit; second, it should make
nitrates which will serve as fertilizer in time of peace
and as the basis of munitions in the time of war. The
manufacture of nitrates of course would not exhaust
the power. The larger part would be available for general manufacturing. Its proper utilization will give the
South that industrial impulse and facility which it
needs. To permit it to be exploited would be a grave
error."

After that people more or less gave up trying to understand the Ford mind, and the Ford Motor Company
went back to the business of making automobiles and
nothing else.

EIGHT

THE BROKEN SONG

T HE Great Depression had revolutionary political and social consequences, some of them irreversible, some of them still acting with unspent force. It began in 1930 and continued like a nightmare of Prometheus in chains until the nation's energies were released again in preparation for World War II. During these ten years the relations between government and people were fundamentally altered. The welfare of people became a direct responsibility of government, whereas always before government was a responsibility of people, and the people minded their own welfare. American ways of thinking and feeling were deeply changed, to the point at which people were willing to surrender personal freedoms and abide compulsions in exchange for a sense of social security.

The song of the wild wheel died suddenly. Even the echoes of it became hateful. In place of it was heard a mighty chorus, led by the voice of the New Deal, demanding that the wheels be tamed, that their revolutions be governed and planned to produce only as much as people could afford to buy at *fair prices*. The delusion was that the wild wheel had caused the depression. It had produced too much, more than people could consume, thereby bringing to pass unemployment and the absurdity of want in the midst of plenty.

No man was more unbelieving than Henry Ford. The popular delusion seized a great majority of the men of business, who were willing to strike hands with government to limit production, restore prices and put competition in a strait jacket; it could not seize him. His mind rejected it completely. But what he would not or could not see was that a world was passing. The delusion was but the furore attending its eclipse; and its eclipse was bound to include him because he was its symbol.

He was still under seventy, and apparently at the peak of his unpredictable powers; nevertheless, his horizons had reversed their direction. Instead of going away they were slowly moving toward him. And as a fateful coincidence, crises in the world of the wild wheel, utterly beyond his control, were parallel in time to crises in the affairs of the Ford Motor Company.

The V-8 was his own last mechanical triumph. As it developed year by year thereafter, to meet competition in style and refinement, fewer ideas came from him and more from the organization, subject to his approval. The authority of his yes and no was final and imperious to the end, but only when it was exercised, and many things went around him. More and more he relied upon

Sorensen, the Magnificent Dane who began as a pattern maker in the Ford shop at three dollars a day and became the great production genius of his time.

It was Sorensen who walked with the rope that pulled the first motorcar assembly line at Highland Park.

It was Sorensen who went to California to see how they made airplanes there, because the Ford Motor Company was going to make them, too, for World War II, and said: "I don't understand this bird's next method." They asked him what he meant by that. He said: "First you build the plane and then you drag everything into it through little holes." They asked him how he would do it. He took the print of a plane and bisected it with lines. "I'd build it in sections, like that," he said, "then stuff the sections and bring them together." That changed the method of airplane construction.

It was Sorensen who said: "You never can forge enough cylinders for the airplanes you want." They asked him how he would make them. He said: "I'd cast them." They said: "That proves what we already knew. Automobile people can't make airplanes. You can cast the cylinders of a motorcar engine but an airplane engine is different." What they were talking about was the lining of an airplane engine cylinder, fitted in the piston well like a membrane that grew there—an exquisite, jewellike thing to look at, absolutely perfect and very slightly tapered because it will expand more at the spark plug end than at the other, which causes

172

it to be precisely true when the engine gets hot. Sorensen went back to the River Rouge plant and cast some
sample cylinders. They were tested under hydraulic
pressure which would rise until they were crushed. The
forged pieces buckled first and crumpled up; the cast
cylinder, when it did buckle, went down like an ac-
cordion hat. After that airplane cylinders were cast,
else, as Sorensen said, there could hardly have been
enough of them, because the forging process is very
slow.

And it was Sorensen who built the famous Willow
Run plant, to produce a bomber an hour, which was the
largest single thing the Ford Motor Company ever did.

2

THE V-8 was brought out in the third year of the
Great Depression. That was bad enough. The obstetri-
cal event was long and painful and entailed a kind of
engineering crisis. This in turn led to a crisis between
the Ford Motor Company and its unhappy dealers, who
again for a long time had nothing to sell and began to
give up.

Ford's complacency at this time astonished his associates. If he thought the superiority of the new car
would sweep the market back to him he was disappointed. Although the V-8 was successful as a car, the
most it could do was to hold the Ford Motor Company
in third place, whereas it had been first. Now it had
become one of the Big Three. The other two were Gen-

173

eral Motors, in first place, and Chrysler in second, who by this time knew as much about automobile making as Ford knew, even more. They were beating him in style and meeting him in price.

Each of his competitors had a line of cars, suited in price to the size of your pocketbook—that is, a low-priced car for the many, a more expensive middle-class car, and then one for the rich. Before the V-8 there had never been anything but a Ford car. When it was the Model T it was the Model T and nothing else. When it was the Model A it was the Model A, take it or leave it. A Ford was a Ford was a Ford.

"No factory," Ford had said, "is large enough to make two kinds of product."

But now he was persuaded that the Ford Motor Company too must have a line of cars. Besides the V-8 there was a six-cylinder car at a lower price, because the dealers wanted it—and the voice of the dealers was beginning for the first time to be respected, for the Ford agency was no longer the little gold mine it had once been. And then there was the Lincoln, which became a Ford product when Ford bought the Lincoln Motor Company. "More for personal reasons," he said, "than because we wanted it. We have no desire to make a commodity of the Lincoln."

Nobody could have made a commodity of the Lincoln. It was in its day the finest and costliest American automobile. Only the rich could afford it. It was designed by Henry M. Leland, whose fame in the motor

world was such that when he organized the Lincoln
Motor Company its capital stock was subscribed in two
hours. At that time Model T was already high on its
way. Leland built his ideal car and it was all that he
meant it to be, but its cost was so high that its market
was bound to be small and it was never a success in a
financial way. Ford bought it to save it from bank-
ruptcy. One of his personal reasons may have been the
desire to have an automobile of that superb quality
within his domain.

The understanding was that the Lincoln Motor Company should continue as a separate province, with
Leland as its vassal lord. Ford did not intend to
cheapen the car, and he never did; he intended only to
reform the manufacturing methods in order to reduce
the cost of producing it. But when his engineers, led by
Sorensen, entered the Lincoln premises and saw how
men worked who had been taught never to worry about
cost they were horrified; on the other side, when these
engineers began to apply Ford methods to eliminate
waste, Leland's blood curdled and he retired with an
embittered heart.

The Lincoln became then a Ford problem. Simply, it
did not lend itself to mass production, which meant that
the price could not be reduced, and if the price could
not be reduced the sales could not be increased. One attempt at solution was to bring out a lower-priced car
called the Lincoln-Zephyr. Then the hyphen was
dropped and there was the Zephyr. Later the Zephyr

disappeared and there was a new Lincoln, still a fine car but not like the old Lincoln and not so costly.

Before the Great Depression the Ford Motor Company's amazing growth, always with its own capital, enabled it to absorb mistakes with astonishing ease. It could write off its white elephants and forget them. So it wrote off a railroad, an excursion into aviation and the Fordson tractor, to mention only three. When it became just another motorcar company, one of the Big Three and in third place, something of that reckless spirit went out of it. However, its essential character never changed. General Motors was a confederacy, Chrysler was a democracy, and both were large borrowers of capital; but the Ford Motor Company was a monarchy so long as Ford lived and a tight family possession after he died, with his grandson, Henry Ford II, on the throne seat.

3

It was in the middle of the Great Depression that the transfer of economic power from the employer to organized labor took place. It took place legally, but in a curious way. The New Deal passed a law under which organized labor was free to enjoy and exercise the power of monopoly—*provided* it had the strength to seize it in open combat with the employer, the government to act as umpire. What followed was a series of bitter struggles on the ground of industry-wide collective bargaining. Organized labor won.

In the motor car industry, as aforesaid, Ford was the most implacable of the Big Three and for that reason the last to be attacked. He was then seventy-five. His defeat was without solace. The union won more than it asked for, and after that the Ford Motor Company was a closed shop; only union members could work there, and Ford became the collector of the members' compulsory union dues, acting for the union treasury.

What he had lost was not just a battle with labor. He had lost his world. Never again would the wheels be wild in a Ford shop. The union would attend to that.

The significance of this change was deeper than anybody knew at the time. Although Ford never expressed it in rational terms he must have known it intuitively.

The one great justification of mass production as he had developed it, for all that might be valid in the resentments of labor, was that it did progressively cheapen the cost of satisfying human wants, so that goods, automobiles or anything else, were ever more abundant and more available, possibly to the point at which sometime they might become as cheap as water carried from the well. But in order for mass production to have that result it was necessary that management should be able to control costs, and management cannot control costs unless it controls both wages and the tempo of work and obeys the hard law of the machine. Here lies the enigma. You may do with it what you like.

In Ford's philosophy, the benefits of mass production were intended for the consumer, which includes labor, since all wage earners are also consumers. In his scheme the consumer was more important than the producer; and if this seems a bit dialectical you may consider the fact that while you may dispense with the wage earner by putting a machine in his place, the consumer, who buys the products of the machine and makes mass production possible, is indispensable. The wage earner is more important in the aspect of consumer than in the aspect of producer, and it follows that in order to be a good consumer he must have high wages.

But when labor itself has the power to say what the wage shall be and how much it will give for the wage received, it claims for itself the first benefits of mass production; the consumer is forgotten. Thus the true economic ends of mass production are defeated, and all you have left is a method of producing goods.

You may say it another way—that the intentions of mass production cannot be realized unless management and labor are both free. So long as that freedom existed in the motorcar industry, the cost of an automobile went lower and lower until it became, pound for pound, the cheapest manufactured thing in the world, not the Ford car only but all cars; and automobile labor at the same time was the highest-paid labor of its kind in the world.

It was estimated that one year Model T generated, directly and indirectly, a payroll of one billion dollars, and that year *the car sold for twenty cents a pound.*

And so we became an automobile people. That could not happen again in a world of tame wheels. If the political and social conditions that now exist had existed in 1900, the American motorcar industry as we know it could not have been created at all.

4

FIVE years after Ford's surrender to organized labor, when he was eighty, his only son, Edsel, died. Tragedy had not touched him before. For more than twenty years Edsel had been president of the Ford Motor Company, a prince regent, acting but not ruling, under the jealous eyes of the king. His story was simple enough. He was the son of a genius. His endless struggle was to get possession of his own life, handicapped by the fact that he was born without a rebellious spirit. The son could not reproduce the father, nor could he be melted down and poured again by the cunning molder who had cast the original V-8 engine block in one piece. Their sympathies were hurt by mutual frustrations of mind and character. Yet in the court of bereavement the judgment was that Edsel's death should be the incomparable loss. Thereafter, all of Ford's days were desolate.

The wealth of the Ford Motor Company at that time was valued at one billion dollars. Who should be president in place of Edsel? Ford was too old; the grandsons were too young. Sorensen was the natural candidate,

179

and it is said that Ford wanted him; yet on second thought he himself resumed the title of president.

Probably the only trouble with Sorensen was that he had got too big. In any case he had got entangled in a maze of jealousies such as can be generated only within a family. Before the end of that year he joined the famous Ford alumni. Ford himself probably did not know exactly how or why it happened. His powers were failing. Harry Bennett, who was his bodyguard, says that after Sorensen was gone Ford would get into the car and say, "Take me over to see Charley," meaning Sorensen. Bennett would say Charley wasn't there any more. Ford would say: "Not there any more. Where is he?"

Nobody has ever been able to explain Harry Bennett's career with the Ford Motor Company. He was a sailor and very handy with his fists. Arthur Brisbane noticed him one morning in a New York dockside brawl, admired his animal qualities, and had the whimsical notion of taking him to Ford, saying, "Here's a man you may be able to use." In an absent manner Ford sent him out to the Highland Park plant, where he had nothing to do and was for a while lost. Over at the new River Rouge plant the superintendent was having some gang trouble and said he needed a big tough guy to deal with it. Bennett was sent over. He introduced himself by knocking down a Polish foreman who asked him what he wanted. He was the tough guy all right, and loved trouble, and became so useful as a persuader of indocile men that he was soon at the head of the internal police. Then Ford began to employ his terrier qualities in curious and devious ways, sometimes to abate trouble and sometimes to create it, the theory of creating it being that executives ought never to be comfortable in their jobs.

In a few years Bennett began to behave as if he were Ford's private Gestapo, as in fact he was; and there came to exist between them a singular intimacy. By exploiting it shrewdly Bennett raised himself to a position of undefined power. Everybody feared him for what he knew or for what he could tell and because his open pathway to Ford was like a secret they shared together, no trespassing allowed. As the years went by and as the shop he could at first hold in one field of vision became an empire that had to be visited, or could be visualized only through the eyes of others, the suspicious side of Ford's nature developed morbidly. Fewer and fewer people could he trust, and the fewer these were the more he trusted Bennett, whose loyalty was exclusive and personal. So it was to the very end. Sorensen could be fired, but not Bennett, unless he fired himself. When at last the family took control, almost the first thing it did was to tell Mr. Bennett good-by and erase his fingerprints wherever they could be found.

Then it began to be said: "If only Bennett would tell what he knows, what a book he could write!" Now Bennett has written his book. Its title is *We Never Called Him Henry*. It is a very stupid book, except as it unconsciously reveals three things, namely: first, that Ford forged Bennett as a mindless tool and then used it with amazing deftness; second, that Bennett had no power at all except as Ford provided it day by day; and, third, that Bennett never knew what Ford was about.

The third point is accounted for by the limitations of Bennett's understanding. If he goes to Heaven he may spend half his eternity with St. Peter and never see in him more than a ticket taker.

5

FORD was a man with no number, no place in any category, no proper explanation. We have seen him acting in the world that passed with him. Shall we leave him there? Or shall we go on to see what he did with that part of his mind which was free of wheels—if it was. At any rate, not the mechanic, not the messenger of mass production, but the man of insatiable wonder to whom everything was new because he did not know any better. For sheer curiosity, let us go on.

NINE

GENIUS IGNORAMUS

F o r d ' s out-shop life had the color, the rich-
ness and somewhat of the dreamlike unreality of a
medieval storybook. Through no fault of his own, only
because he is somehow different, the hero is misunder-
stood and ridiculed by his own people, who seem to
forget how much they are indebted to him for the works
he has performed in their service; he sets out on a jour-
ney into strange lands, with a stick in his hands that
turns out to be a magic wand; he has many exciting ex-
periences and returns with pageantry in his train and
forgivingness in his heart and builds them for free a
Wonder Place, which they enjoy to this day.

It began when an editorial writer on the Chicago
Tribune called him an ignoramus. He sued the newspaper for libel, asking damages in the sum of one million
dollars.

The trial took place at Mt. Clemens, Michigan. It
was an American event, purely native, unimaginable in
any other jungle of civilization, except possibly in
comic opera. The only person not paid to do it who

183

took it seriously was Ford himself. People at large were immensely tickled by the spectacle of the world's most original and most successful industrialist undergoing a teen-age intelligence test, in a country courtroom before a rural jury, at the hands of pompous lawyers who behaved as the sheriffs of knowledge and used the dictionary as a book of wisdom. The little town was overcome by its sudden importance. Its inhabitants were as dazed as if they had stumbled onto a movie set and were groping in the limelight, stepping on parts of the apparatus and colliding with celebrities.

The news was covered with fine journalistic frenzy. Reporters working in relays were continually rushing to the telephone with bulletins for the headlines:

Ford says, "I don't know what you mean by fundamental principles of government."

Ford guesses he forgot the War of Independence.

Ford says the War of 1812 was a revolution.

Ford doesn't know who Benedict Arnold was.

Ford says he can read but refuses to try.

And so on and on for weeks.

The absurdity of it was painful. His answers were sometimes sullen, sometimes angry when his tormentors pushed him too far, and then again so unexpectedly satirical and so barbed with common sense that the pomposities were shattered. What was the United States in the beginning? "Land," he said. And once, instead of saying again that he didn't know, he said, as he whittled the sole of his shoe: "I can find somebody to tell me in five minutes all I want to know about that." His ignorance of history was probably shared by some members of the jury. He was a better witness than he knew. His performance did him no damage whatever in public esteem; on the contrary, his simplicity, his earthiness, the weariness of his contempt for the magniloquent word, his un-self-saving candor about what he had never had time to learn from books, endeared him to millions, all more or less like that themselves, only ashamed to confess it.

Nevertheless, it was an ordeal. He had not foreseen it. He learned something about the savagery of litigation when counsel for the Chicago *Tribune*, in his summing up, said: "Gentlemen of the jury, they forced us to open the mind of Henry Ford and expose it to you bare, to disclose the pitiable condition that he had succeeded in keeping from the view of the public."

The jury found the Chicago *Tribune* guilty of libel, and Ford was awarded damages in the sum of six cents.

2

THE verdict of course was worthless. He was hurt and humiliated, and for all the rest of his life he was doing something about it, even long after the hurt was gone.

His first answer was to start the Dearborn *Independent*, a weekly magazine, the leading feature of which was "Mr. Ford's Own Page." He didn't write it, of course, but the ideas were his. Then in collaboration with Samuel Crowther he did three books—and very interesting books they were. After that, who could say he was an ignoramus?

A saying that kept coming back to plague him was: "History is bunk." It took him a long time to learn that an ignoramus may not say such a thing out loud, but a scholar, even an historian, may say it. Van Loon opened his *History of Mankind* with those words, and that was all right.

Years later I was a customer in the Ford Hospital in Detroit. It had become my favorite service station. Cameron came in to see me. He asked me if there was anything I wanted to read. I said I had been intending the next time I was in bed to read "The Yale Chronicles," but I hadn't been able to find them in Detroit. He said: "We've got them in our library." The next day they came, fifty volumes in a wooden box. The first title I picked up was *Elizabethan Sea Dogs*, by William Wood. There I read how Henry VIII, whose best friends were his sailormen, found Fletcher of Rye, who had discovered the art of tacking and could sail a ship against the wind. The whole king's navy was made over on that new principle, and the next time it went into battle it confounded the enemy by sailing around him in zigzag patterns, no matter where the wind was, killing him with broadsides. That was the foundation of British sea power.

I had just put the book down when Ford came in. He asked what I was reading and I told him the story.

186

Then I added: "Think how much history you might have read without coming on that one simple tremendous fact." His eyes lighted as he tapped me on the knee and said: "Yes, history is bunk, as I always said it was."

He could say it then with ease and surety, for in the years between he had done something with American history.

He had seized it by its artifacts and put it in a showcase.

That was his answer to the jeering he took when he first said history was bunk.

3

HE EXPLORED the past as if it were an unknown world, pushing off like a boy on a raft, with no destination and only a yesterly sense of direction—this man who had never been a boy because he was born with his head full of wheels. It was a dream raft that stopped of itself when he said, "There! What's that?" And it was a wonderful world, in one way especially, that it stirred in him the kind of remembrance you may have of things that have happened but did not happen to you. Each time he returned to the raft he brought some curious object that was new because it was old. When the raft was full he needed a barge and when the barge was full a string of barges, and then trains, ships, planes and fleets of motor vehicles to send the things back.

What were they, these things? Anything at all, any

relic of the ancestral life; and the ancestral life was all
the life that had been lived before Model T. Later he
said: "We want to have something of everything." So
it might be a windmill, a buggy, a string of sleigh bells,
a rusty reaper, a stern-wheel river boat, old pots and
pans, a log cabin, wooden Indians, furniture, crockery,
a crazy quilt, fiddles, a cradle, a chair somebody sat in
—and not one of each kind of thing but many, hundreds, even thousands.

The wand was not money. It was a physical power
to externalize fantasy. That was a power that could
no more have been evolved by money alone than an organization to produce an automobile every ten seconds.

What Ford had behind him was a self-contained
cosmos out of which, at a moment's notice, he could call
a team of engineers, mechanics and seabees to do anything. When he called they came running with the right
tools in their hands. Anything he could think of, that
they could do, and do it the Ford way with a kind of
military urgency. It might be something nobody ever
heard of before until the call came, or something nobody had ever done before. Sometimes it required a kind
of forgotten skill. In that case somebody riffled the employee cards showing what a man did before he became
a Ford machine worker, and nearly always the skill was
there, or even the talent, one instance being that of a
young Hungarian who knew what a cymbalum was and
how to play it and was transferred from the shop to the

188

Ford dance band. He had only to say, "Do this," and it was done before he could get back to see. Besides, in the extremely rare case, if he stumped them he could tell them how. Certainly men who made a chore of picking up bodily a tractor plant in Detroit and setting it down in Ireland would make no difficulty at all of such a task as to take down an old stone cottage in Cotswold, England, stone by stone in numbered bags, and set it up again in Dearborn, so perfectly that when the authentic landscaping was added the English masons who came along to do the work had moments of thinking they dreamed it. This Cotswold cottage was a freak whim. The only notion to justify it in Greenfield Village —which is coming—was that Americans might like to see how their ancestors were housed before they came to this country.

4

HE ACCUMULATED an incredible quantity of Americana. Some of it was good; a lot of it was debris. To find it he searched attics, cellars, dumps, junk yards, secondhand stores, antique shops, barn lots, hillsides, crossroad hamlets, all the eddies and backwaters of a by-gone life. Yet he was not a collector. As we use the word, a collector is one who collects objects of a certain kind in a certain order; it may be paintings, first editions, rare bindings, porcelains, glass, weapons, period furniture, historical documents, coins, stamps, even trifling things such as buttons or paper match books; the interest may be aesthetic or whimsical, but always selective.

There is no word for a collector who collects everything. It is something else he is doing.

For example, when Ford discovered the *McGuffey Readers* there were already a number of fine collections of that piece of Americana, in the hands of bibliophiles who had spent years getting together the complete series, who knew one another as fellow hobbyists, swapped books to fill in gaps and exchanged information. Ford was not content to have such a collection; it was not enough to reproduce the books in beautiful facsimile and distribute them privately; but he must have the log cabin in which William Holmes McGuffey was born on a western Pennsylvania farm, and then a replica of the schoolhouse where he taught, built of logs cut on the farm where he was born, together with the desk he used. Or if Lincoln was his discovery, then besides the kind of Lincolniana a discriminating collector would pursue, such as papers, books, documents and letters, he must have from Illinois the Logan County Court House where Lincoln practiced law—the building itself—and in it, according to the words of the Greenfield Village *Guide Book*, "several pieces of Lincoln furniture, the original corner cupboard fashioned by young Abe and his father, Lincoln's wardrobe, the table from a law office where he once practiced, a number of chairs and other pieces from his Springfield home, and

190

in one corner the chair in which he was seated in the box of a Washington theatre on the night of his assassination"—and a fireplace like the one that was probably there and on the hearth an eternal flame lighted by President Hoover.

Not objects of any order, not objects in any sequence, not objects for sheer love of them, although in *My Life and Work* he did say: "Our forefathers knew how to order some parts of their lives better than we do. They had much better taste; they knew more about beauty in the design of commonplace, everyday things." That dim rationalization of the fantasy was probably phrased by Samuel Crowther.

What was he trying to collect? The past. Simply that.

The past cannot be a collector's item. But if you are trying to put it in the eye of dull imagination, you may need such things as a Pennsylvania Dutch churn, an old vertical steam engine, the first Edison phonograph or Georgia slave huts authentically reproduced in brick from a brickyard on the plantation where Negro slaves did actually live.

The further he went with it the more it absorbed him until his actions seemed to proceed from a source of inner compulsion, and he came to be seized with a great nostalgia for a way of life that had been destroyed by electricity, the internal-combustion engine and automobiles.

He hated the drudgery of farm life and fled from it;

he thought he had done more than any other man to relieve it. He wrote: "I have followed many a weary mile behind a plow and I know all the drudgery of it. What a waste it is for a human being to spend hours and days behind a slowly moving team of horses when in the same time a tractor could do six times as much work!" When he went back to the land it was with tractors. He had a large dairy farm in Dearborn. It delighted him to watch there fifty tractors plowing in line. That was farming. "Our dairy farm," he said, "is managed exactly like a factory."

All the same he loved the old way too. In another mood he said: "It was an evil day when the village flour mill disappeared."

When the things he had sent back from the world of the past made a pile so high and wide that it was in the way, even on the spacious River Rouge premises, and something had to be done about it, the thought of a museum began to take form. But a museum could be only a partial solution. For how could you put an old church, steeple and all, indoors on the teakwood floor of a museum? Well, anybody might have thought of the natural answer to that. There had to be an outdoor museum, too, something like an old-fashioned village, with a green in the middle and around the green all the things proper to a village—things that would be there if it were a real village and not the ghost of one.

TEN

HISTORY'S REVENGE

T H E museum first. It had to have a name; and it was named the Edison Institute Museum, to express Ford's affection for his great friend the wizard. Then it had to have a front elevation, nothing modern, something in the way of colonial architecture, yet as grand as possible.

So now as you approach it you will see in replica not one but three historic Philadelphia buildings joined as one façade—Independence Hall, Congress Hall and the old City Hall. As you enter you have at your right a reproduction of the room in which the Declaration of Independence was signed, and on your left a reproduction of what was the chamber of the first United States Supreme Court.

In this vicinity, as if you might want to see them first, or because there was no place else to put them, are the art exhibits, such as you would find in any museum— examples of fine furniture, ceramics, silver, glass, bits of exquisite workmanship in metals and fabrics and wood, many decorative objects, some of them with his-

193

tories attached—but no paintings. Somebody may tell you that Mr. Ford did not find paintings very interesting. He had once said he did not care a nickel's worth for all the paintings in the world.

Go straight on and you come to the Main Exhibition Hall. As much of the fantasy as could make itself manifest begins there.

The *Guide Book* will tell you that Mr. Ford expressed his aims as follows: "When we are through we shall have reproduced American life as lived; and that, I think, is the best way of preserving at least a part of our history and tradition. For by looking at things people used and that show the way they lived, a better and truer impression can be gained than could be had in a month of reading—even if there were books whose authors had the facilities to discover the minute details of the older life."

Main Street is over there.

You may not remember what Main Street was like in your grandfather's time. Over the shops, called both shops and stores, were emblems of the trade—for the tinware shop a giant coffeepot, for the shoe store a gilded boot, for the jeweler a dummy watch the size of a center table top, and so on. Well, here it is. It is an illusion, and yet all the properties are real; and the people who play at keeping store or at making things as if they might be for sale if they ever get finished—they are real too. There is the harness shop and a man making harness and out in front the full-sized effigy of a dapple-gray horse. There is the barbershop, with one chair, individual shaving mugs on the shelf, water heating in a copper tank on a coal stove, and a barber with unfortunately nothing to do, because a shave and haircut, unlike a set of harness, cannot be hung on a peg at night and taken down again in the morning to be worked on during museum hours. Then a tobacco store with a wooden Indian outside, a tailor shop with out-of-style garments in the window, a boot and shoe store, a millinery and fancy-goods shop, a corner drugstore with the old urn-shaped bottles of colored water in the window, a comb shop equipped with the authentic tools of the comb-making craft, a fiddle shop and a toy store. When you come to the end of the street you can walk back on the other side, passing the gun maker, the candlestick maker, the cabinetmaker and the wheelwright. The scene generally speaking is New England, and so there is Gurdlestone & Sons, East India merchants, with ship models, chests and nautical curiosities scattered about, just as they might have been on the business premises of a Yankee firm in the clipper ship trade; and at the end of the street, where it should be, a reconstruction of the Caleb Taft blacksmith shop which Longfellow knew, equipped with a bellows forge, nail makers' benches and the ox sling that did actually lift the ox off its feet to be shod.

You have missed a great deal, but if you are going to get through your eyes the equivalent of a month's reading you must not dawdle too long in Main Street.

There is a section devoted to agriculture. There you will see nearly every kind of tool man has ever plowed the ground with, at least back to ancient Egyptian times, and nearly every kind of device with which he has reaped the harvest, and then the instruments for threshing and winnowing, from great antiquity down to the appearance not so long ago of power-driven farm machinery, and the very steam engine used by Henry Ford in the threshing season in 1882, when he was nineteen and still soil-bound.

And there too you will see that man has long been an ingenious animal and thoughtful of his wife, for here are the little dog treadmills he made to turn her churn, so that instead of wearing herself out with the churn plunger she could be doing something else while the dog made the butter. That would have been a high-class farmer only; most of them let their wives make butter the hard way, and there are the churns to prove it, nearly every kind of hand churn there ever was, with plungers, rollers or paddles. The butter was for bread. Baking was the woman's job. But man made the flour, and here are flour-milling inventions all the way back to the wooden mortar and pestle used by the American Indian while the advanced people of Europe were already using water-power gristmills, like the one you are looking at.

The next section is given to textiles and household arts. How did people clothe themselves before there

196

were any mail-order catalogues? Here are the tools and implements they actually used with their hands, back to the tenth century—a crude cotton gin, flax breakers, spinning wheels, early examples of the spinning jenny from Wales, looms that made gingham and linsey-woolsey, a Chinese loom, a Dutch loom, one of the first Singer sewing machines, poke bonnets, and how they made their hats. And then the woman's own tools, such, according to the *Guide Book*, as "carpet stretchers, niddy-noodies, lace bobbins, knee looms, old scissors, flat irons, ironing boards, mangles, washing boards, washtubs, washing machines and fluting irons."

The section devoted to manufacture is entirely inhabited by old steam engines, beginning with a Newcomen engine, built in 1760, that ran continuously for seventy years to pump the water out of a coal mine in England, then lay on the junk pile for one hundred years, until the Earl of Stamford graciously presented it to the museum in 1930. Near it is one of the first Watt engines that also worked itself out in England—and then engines, engines as far as your eye can see, arranged more or less in the line of their evolution through three hundred years of steam power. One group of twenty is made up of steam engines for the farmer—clumsy ancestors of the tractor—and one of these bears the following note: "A Monitor portable engine, made at Ypsilanti, Michigan, vertical fire box, horizontal boiler attached at the top. A sapling which had grown through the spokes of the wheels during the years it stood in disuse was cut off at the base and remains entwined in the wheel."

Electricity is next. Electricity suggests artificial light. There is a display of eleven hundred electric light bulbs, from one the size of a grain of wheat to one that weighs thirty-six pounds; but then, speaking of artificial light, here are Eskimo lamps, ancient clay lamps, whale oil lamps, hanging and swinging and petticoat lamps, candles, rush lights, chandeliers, candlesticks, snuffers, trays and matchholders. Electricity then suggests the vacuum cleaner and what was before that, for example, the Brussels carpet sweeper and before that the straw broom and before that the homemade brushes of the Colonists. "Modern heating and cooking devices," says the *Guide Book*, "have evolved from gas equipment and kerosene, and back through early base burners, the Franklin stove and the open fire place"—as you can see for yourself. How electricity could have suggested printing is not clear. Perhaps it didn't. Anyhow here it is—models of the wooden hand press of Blaue, the Columbian hand press, the Washington hand press, etc., "with representative products of the printing art." Also here a section of every cable that was ever laid across the floor of the Atlantic.

Now you will have to hurry through transportation. But for the distraction of Main Street you might have started with the wheels. Here is nearly every way man has thought of moving himself and his burdens on wheels, in model, in replica and whenever possible the thing itself, from the reproduction of a two-wheeled chariot found in the tomb of Tutankhamen, through ox carts, a carriage from Russia, fancy horse-drawn vehicles from old Europe, every kind of American horse-drawn vehicle, including the Nancy Hanks sulky, a band wagon, the Hotel Del Monte bus which was the largest bus ever built, a gypsy wagon, butcher wagons, fire engines, a circus calliope, a Japanese jinrikisha, bicycles and velocipedes, all the way down to the time when mechanical power began to be added to the wheels, and from there on locomotives, railroad trains and automobiles. At the beginning of the automobile section is the first three-color highway traffic signal in the world; also the first gasoline service station.

The evolution of the Ford automobile is made visible, model by model, and there also is old "999," Ford's famous racing car. You will see cars that were overcome by the Ford in competition, some that were not, some with forgotten names that were famous in their time, such as an old Pierce-Arrow, a Stanley Steamer and the air-cooled Franklin that died in spite of its fans. There is also "the Lincoln that transported King George VI and Queen Elizabeth during their historic visit to this continent."

If you were expecting a visualized history of the American automobile, complete and authentic from the beginning, it is not here. Only the story of the Ford is complete; the rest of it is a miscellany of old cars. In some of them are figures which, says the *Guide Book*, are "dressed to period in dusters, veils and black leather gauntlets."

And all of this on a teakwood floor laid in herringbone design on mastic, to last forever. Teakwood is logged out of the jungles of Asia by elephant power. Ford loved teakwood and used a great deal of it.

Greenfield Village is outside. There you walk or maybe you will be picked up by a horse-drawn bus. Automobiles are forbidden.

2

IF YOU can imagine a storybook coming to life, so that the things you are supposed to see with the mind's eye become visible to the sensory eye, tangible, full size, in three-dimensional form, and arrange themselves becomingly in a park, then you may have some notion of what Greenfield Village is like. Everything is either its original self or a reproduction so true that it might as well be—or, at the very least, it is made of the same materials as the original or materials from that very place. There are eighty-six structures, each with some legend or history about it, or, if not, then a forethought of verisimilitude, as in the case of the blacksmith shop where the anvil rings, the sparks fly and the sweating smith works his bellows forge, standing, says the *Guide Book*, "in the shade of a spreading chestnut tree, as did the one made famous by the poet Longfellow."

From the veranda of Clinton Inn you may look up and down the Village Green.

Before railroads, Clinton Inn was the first overnight stop on your way from Detroit to Chicago by stage-coach. It was brought here in a dilapidated condition and restored to live a second life. The taproom is dry. Otherwise it is all as much the way it was as anybody could imagine, with its rag carpets, horsehair furniture in the parlor, lace curtains, a three-candle ratchet chandelier from the central ceiling beam, the fireplaces, old bottles and old prints.

To your left is the Chapel of Mary and Martha. The bell in the steeple was cast by Paul Revere, Jr. The *Guide Book* tells you that "the bricks in the building and the doors are from the girlhood home of Mrs. Henry Ford"—and it seems to have no other historical importance, except as rather a fine facsimile of an old New England church.

The garden between the inn and the church is said to be "a replica of an herb garden in Greece in the thirteenth century," and the only explanation of it is that it is "an expression of Mrs. Henry Ford's interest in herb gardening." The name of it is the "Garden of the Leavening Heart."

In all sweetness, why not? Any collector may have this experience. His wife comes with something that doesn't belong and says, "I'd like to put this here." And besides, how could he say no to a thirteenth-century Grecian herb garden when he himself had brought to Greenfield

201

Village the Sir John Bennett Jewelry Shop from Cheapside, London, with some of the original façade and certainly the original giants Gog and Magog, striking the quarter hours with hammers, only because it touched his fancy?

But what are these two black cylindrical objects against the sky, a little to the right of the church steeple? If you were old enough to remember you would say they were the twin smokestacks of the kind of sternwheeler that used to navigate American rivers. You would be right. That is what they are. Over there is a circular artificial lagoon named the Suwanee River, since it could be named anything, and riding on the captive water is a real stern-wheeler, sometimes with steam up, also named *Suwanee*.

All of that is backdrop. Ford had a strong sentimental weakness for the old folk songs of Stephen C. Foster and a particular fondness for "The Old Folks at Home," with the refrain, "Way down upon the Suwanee River." He acquired the house in which Foster was supposed to have been born and had the notion, besides, of keeping in it an everlasting flame lighted by the hand of a lineal descendant. The *Guide Book* expects you to be thrilled as your eyes rest upon an association of objects described as follows: "The stern wheeler Suwanee floats on the quiet waters of the Suwanee River in the valley just northeast of the Village Green. Stephen Foster's house overlooks the lagoon bearing the name of the river his song made famous."

3

You are still on the veranda of Clinton Inn. The bell in the steeple rings. From the little red schoolhouse on the other side of the green children spill out and come toward you. They will have lunch at the inn.

The village maintains an educational system, complete from kindergarten to high school. Several buildings are devoted to that use. The one you are looking at across the green—the one the children are coming from—is the Scotch Settlement School, where Ford learned his ABC's. It is just as it was then—the old-fashioned stove, kerosene lamps, the old blackboards, the old desks with hearts and boy-and-girl initials carved on them by stealthy jackknives, and the organ. Modern lighting, heating and ventilation have been installed, but all such contraptions are concealed so as not to spoil the antique effect. There is another school on the green, and a third one a little way off, and then at some distance the Noah Webster house, where, instead of learning home economics out of books, groups of girls take turns at keeping house. This Noah Webster house, where the lexicographer wrote his dictionary, stood on the campus of Yale University until it had to make room for modern buildings; then the wreck of it was brought here for resurrection.

Some of the buildings in the Edison group were resurrected, that is, the pieces were recovered from dumps and salvage yards and put together; some were carefully dismembered where they stood and raised again here. Therefore, it is all original—the laboratory where Edison explored the properties of matter, his office and library, his glass house where the first incandescent light bulbs were blown, his machine shop, the carpenter shop, and even Sarah Jordan's boardinghouse, where some of the Edison workers lived. One day they strung some wires from the machine shop to Sarah's place, and that made it historic as the first house ever to be lighted by electricity. The *Guide Book* asks you to notice that these Edison buildings stand on reddish soil, unlike the black soil of Michigan; and this, it explains, "is due to the fact that Mr. Ford has surrounded the buildings with soil from Menlo Park, New Jersey," that is, the very soil on which they were built in the first place.

A little way off, as it had to be, is the Smith's Creek Depot. It was bought from the Grand Trunk Railroad, taken down brick by brick and rebuilt here, platform and all, because that was where one night a young news butcher named Thomas A. Edison was thrown off the train after having caused a fire by spilling some acid out of his portable chemical laboratory. There is a piece of railroad track in front of it, and when Golden Light's Jubilee was celebrated in 1929 the funny old Grand Trunk train itself chuffed up to the depot. President Hoover came out of it, with Edison by the arm, and "led him," says the *Guide Book*, "to the same platform on which he had been deposited by the conductor sixty-seven years earlier."

204

4

W I L L you take a walk?

You may want to see the house where William Holmes
McGuffey was born, appointed with "McGuffey furniture," or the Logan County Court House, where Abra-
ham Lincoln practiced law and where the everlasting
flame in the fireplace was lighted by President Hoover;
or the house where Orville Wright was born, and beside
it the Wright Bicycle Shop where the brothers made
bicycles before they made the first successful flying machine; or the birthplace of Henry Ford, an old farmhouse with the original steel windmill; or some log cabins
in authentic reproduction and the Georgia slave huts.

If you are interested in the economic activities of ye
olden time you will want to see the general store, exactly as it was in 1854 at Waterford, Michigan, with
"the original counters, spice and coffee grinders, cracker
barrels, hoop skirts, fancy jewelry, skates and comic
valentines"; and the old apothecary shop, with its wood
stove, herb drawers, drug bottles and jars for leeches;
and the tintype studio, with tintypes of many famous
modern persons on the walls, who sat for fun; and the
cooper shop where a cooper could go right to work on
his hoops and staves; and the Sandwich glass shop from
Massachusetts; a tile works, a pottery, a gristmill, a
weave shed, a cotton gin, a sawmill, a cider mill, a planing mill, a sorghum molasses mill, a carriage shop, a
Cape Cod windmill of the Dutch type, and a reproduc-
205

tion of the first power plant of the Edison Illuminating Company of Detroit, where Henry Ford worked as an engineer for forty dollars a month and where in his spare time he made his first automobile.

You may have missed the Cotswold Cottage, brought from England, and the Floral Clock, of which the *Guide Book* says: "It used to stand at the entrance of Waterworks Park. The works originally were turned by water power, but were never very efficient. When they became so inefficient that it was decided to destroy the old landmark, Mr. Ford brought it to Greenfield Village. One family of plants makes up the dial. Telanthera in various colors are used in the design of both the border of the innermost circle of the dial and the outside border, as well as the large center star. Several thousand plants are in the dial, and require constant watering and trimming. They are imbedded in soil six inches deep held in place by chicken wire. During the winter the plants are replaced by a painted replica."

On the way back to the green you will pass the Toll House Shoe Shop. It was built in 1828 at one end of a covered bridge between Rocks Village and West Newbury on the Merrimack River. The *Guide Book* says: "John Greenleaf Whittier was fond of sitting in the shop. He wrote in 'The Countess' of 'the tollman in his cobbler's stall.' The first toll collector made shoes as a side line and each succeeding collector followed that trade. Today one hears the shoemaker's hammer from the little shop, but no longer does its wielder collect a fare from travelers. Inside are many little things of interest—a rabbit gun, a telescope, the cobbler's violin and shelves filled with shoes made by the craftsman working there."

And it would be too bad if you had missed the Village Fire Department. Over the doorway is the word *Deluge*. The engine, says the *Guide Book*, "is of the suction type, built in 1845 by the Hunneman Fire Engine Works for Rocks Village, Mass." On the walls are examples of the capes, belts and hats the volunteer firemen wore, and their decorated buckets; and the small white pine building enclosing all of this once housed the village hearse of Newton, New Hampshire. The hearse is forever lost.

As the Ford Motor Company was Ford's personal tool, so Greenfield Village was his personal toy. Both were in his native landscape, from which he never departed; and both in a curious way were manifestations of the same spirit. But whereas the tool was disciplined by the pure logic of function, the toy was anything he imagined it to be. It was the one thing he ever made that did not have to work. He thought he was creating the image of a life he had done more to destroy than any other man of his time.

History had its revenge. The man who had said history was bunk, not knowing any better, came to be fascinated by any object that had a history, so only it was something he could touch. Current time claimed his mind and the future his imagination, but his heart belonged to the past.

Emotionally he was an incurable rustic, with a smell of the soil about him and a touch of clownishness in moments of impulsive behavior. Once he arrived very late at a dinner where some tycoons were solemnly waiting and astonished them by taking the top of the table in one long-legged stride and kicking the chandelier. As he sat down he was the only one in the room not in the least embarrassed. He was late one morning to keep an appointment with the editor of the Manchester *Guardian* at the chapel in Greenfield Village. When he appeared he was leaping up the steps like a tardy schoolboy. The editor said: "Why do you do that, a man of your age?" He grinned and said: "Just to show off."

5

OLD inns enchanted him. A beautiful one at South Sudbury, Massachusetts, cast its spell upon him at sight, and he bought it. When with lavish pains he had completely restored its olden character there was still one thing that seemed very wrong. The highway in front of it was full of disrespectful automobile traffic. The fact that most of the automobiles were Fords did nothing to soften the discordant note. It was easier to move the highway than to uproot the inn. So he moved the highway out of sight and sound, by leave of the State of Massachusetts, if he would bear the entire cost, which he did.

By this time there was almost no scar tissue left from

his humiliation at Mt. Clements, where in his libel suit against the Chicago *Tribune* his ignorance of Colonial events had exposed him to ridicule, for now he could regard himself as the patron of New England history.

Was not the Wayside Inn a vanishing historical memento that ought to be preserved? Washington must have known its hospitality, and Lafayette, and Longfellow had enshrined it in his *Tales of a Wayside Inn*.

His first intention was limited. He would restore it to its original character and leave it to the public as an heirloom.

Besides doing the things that anyone might have thought of, such as to open the sixteen fireplaces that had been sealed up, to put in electric lights that looked like candles, and to make the furnishings completely and authentically Colonial, he searched the country for relics that had disappeared. One old trunk was traced to Kansas and brought back. The clock, dated 1710, got new insides and was made to run and keep time, with the worn-out parts, such as wooden gears, preserved in a glass case for anyone who wanted to see what the work of the old clock makers was like. The old Bible was lovingly repaired and then locked up in a glass case, for the eye only.

Then the intention began to grow. The native life that had surrounded the Wayside Inn—that also should be restored. So he bought the whole neighborhood. The idea now was to create not a museum of dead things but a working demonstration of life as it transacted itself in Revolutionary times. There was a rickety old grist-mill with an undershot water wheel that was feebly grinding only feed. That was made into a flour mill again, just as it was in, say, 1776, with an efficient over-shot wheel, to grind wheat and rye and corn. How did they grow their wheat and rye and corn in those days? That was something to be demonstrated. Old plows and rude farming tools were found and put back to work on the soil, with oxen to draw them. Also sawmills, forges and blacksmith shops, all working again, like the clock in the inn. And everything but the clock turning anti-clockwise in time.

It behooved us, he said, to look backward; not only to know but actually to see how our forebears made way and what life was like before machines. He did not mean simply that if we kept reminding ourselves of the con-trast and made it vivid to our senses we should be able to appreciate the present more, instead of taking it so much for granted. Not that at all. He said again and again that from the rise of modern industry life had suffered a positive loss. The gains, to be sure, were immensely greater than the loss; nevertheless, we should not forget the loss nor undervalue it. By not forgetting it, by keeping the sense of it alive, we could be more hopeful of sometime finding a way both to keep the gains and retrieve the loss. Yet he never could quite define what the loss was. He only felt it. The fact was that he came to have an aching nostalgia for village industry and for life as it was before machines and mass production. Or was it that he had an unconscious sense of guilt at having done more than any other one man to destroy idyllic existence?

Here at any rate lies the peak of contradiction. In the mood induced by the celestial clangor of River Rouge he could think all bucolic animals absurd and obsolete, even the cow. In the mood induced by Wayside Inn he could think there was something to be learned by putting oxen back to work on the soil.

6

ONE of his late discoveries was old-fashioned dancing, for which he organized classes, hired teachers, invented an orchestra around a dulcimer and a cymbalum from Budapest, searched the backwoods for old fiddle players who could remember both the words and the tunes, provided a teakwood floor in the Engineering Laboratory at Dearborn, and wrote a severe book of rules.

Finding the old fiddlers was an exciting pastime. He would hear of one here and another one there and he would go himself to inveigle them. One day he gathered up his doctor companion, Roy McClure, saying: "Come on. I've heard of a good one." It was a long drive into the country. On the way he said: "It will probably be a little farmhouse. The woman won't be expecting us, and yet nothing will do but she must feed us. Let's feed her." At the next town they stopped at a hardware store and got something that would do for a grill and at the butcher's for some steaks and at a grocery store for salt and pepper and bread and butter. When they arrived the fiddler was not at home and Ford astonished the woman by asking her not to send for him but to eat with them while they waited. He made a fire, got some green corn out of the field and cooked a very good dinner. This he loved to do. It reminded him of the muskrat stew he cooked on the ice at the end of his race in the "999." So the ancient fiddler found them when he returned to his rooftree, his own woman enlisted on the side of the strangers, and there was no escape.

Ford's delight in his forty fiddlers, especially one who at eighty-five could dance and fiddle at the same time, gave his new fantasy the necessary touch of incongruity. He tingled to lively folk tunes and had a feeling in his feet for the hillbilly capering that went with them; but his serious intention was to restore old-fashioned dancing in true and elegant form.

The idea came to him suddenly as he gazed at what had been a fine Colonial ballroom in the Wayside Inn. His imagination re-created there the stately scenes of a past time, such as he may have seen prints of in New England albums and scrapbooks, the gallants and their ladies treading the rhythmic measures, perhaps even Lafayette himself in this very place, all behaving in a grand and formal manner. This he compared with modern dancing, to jazz music, not in ballrooms but in huddling places, and his resolve was made. Life had lost its most charming and graceful adornment. He would bring it back.

He went about it with vestiges of the Model T spirit. First the ballroom, partitioned off on the teakwood floor of the Engineering Laboratory at Dearborn, big enough for seventy couples. That was the chassis. Then an orchestra which he designed himself. That was the power plant. Then a search for suitable old music. That would be the ignition system. After that a book of rules as rigid as the old Ford manual that went with every Model T, so that every man might be his own mechanic. Everybody had to dance in absolutely the correct way. It was all there in the book, and the reason for it was that what made old-fashioned dancing so attractive was the deportment. There could be no cutting in. It was forbidden for ladies to enter the ballroom without escort; the ladies must slightly precede the gentlemen. No one under any circumstances should cross the center of the dance floor.

But what of the customers? Dancing, like everything else, had to attract customers and satisfy them, else you might know there was something wrong with the product. Here was no question of price. It was all free. Yet two difficulties appeared. The only people who could remember the old dances thought they were too old to dance and the young people who liked to dance had never heard of them. Well, then, he would teach them—the old to dance again and the young to learn how. For that he needed dancing masters and classes, both of which he provided; and the bi-weekly dance night at the Engineering Laboratory became the affair

213

most *de rigueur* in the social life of Detroit. One effect, probably not intended, was to soften the old and bitter feud between the Philistinism of Dearborn and the aristocracy of Grosse Pointe. The very best people came. The passing generation had mellowed and was forgetful; the new generation was too bored to care what the quarrel had been about.

Ford said no one ever objected to the formality. They liked it. Certainly. It was implicit in the book of rules that you had to like it. For Ford executives and their wives an invitation was like a royal command. The Grosse Pointers had reasons of their own for coming. In any case, the groaning was done at home, before and after. Ford never heard it.

As a cultural renascence it turned out to be a brave little flame from dying embers. Not a trace of it survives.

7

IF HE had been born a hillbilly, with no wheels in his head, he might have been a fine whittler. One day on his Georgia plantation he was showing some guests a new sawmill. Suddenly he left them sitting on a log and vanished into the mill, and was gone so long that they felt obliged to go looking for him. They found him whittling the wooden handle of a control lever. He was just finishing. "See," he said, "how much better it is now. How it fits the hand."

A little later in the house he uncovered for them the

secret model of a new engine. For years the idea of a five-cylinder engine had been tormenting him, because for one reason his engineers said it was not feasible, and he had been working on it here. The engine was still wrong, but the handle he had just whittled was perfect. As he whittled he was probably not thinking about the engine; yet, according to his theory, something about the engine might have popped into his head while his hands were busy with the jackknife. Certainly nothing could ever happen to you while your hands were still.

Life and work and play all as one thing, like a three-ply thread, until the mysterious weaver has used it up and the end runs off the empty spool. On the night of that terminal event a terrific storm broke upon Dearborn and the wonderful Edisonian world was blocked out while Henry Ford died by the light of a coal oil lamp.

ENVOY

I T IS customary in the beginning to say why one is going to write a book. That was done. If at the end it is not clear there is very little that can be done about it. The theme was Laissez Faire, the subject was Henry Ford, and the idea was to illustrate the theme by means of the subject, so that one might say,

Man hath the design of his time.

There was the promise in the Foreword that there should be no moral judgment. Simply, for better or worse, it was like that. Let the reader do with it what he will.

It was a world many people grew not to want, or wanted so little that they were unwilling to defend it. Only the strong could love it. Anyhow, it is gone. The number of those who knew it is rapidly dwindling. In a little while nobody living will be able to remember it at all. For that reason the book is not round if it omits to say wherein it differed from the world we now have.

The first condition in it was freedom of the human will—freedom in all dimensions. What a man would,

216

that he could—if he could, provided only he did not cross the right of another to do likewise.

The only law he had to think about was one forbidding him to restrain trade by conspiracy, and that was something Ford never had the slightest intention of doing. He was a complete individualist.

There was no Federal Trade Commission to mind his way of doing business.

Taxes were nominal. There was no progressive taxation to penalize growth or bigness. If a man made a dollar it was all his own.

There was no law to compel him to bargain collectively with union labor. There was no law requiring him to recognize unions.

Wages were determined, not by the employer, as the saying was, but by the law of supply and demand acting in a free labor market. The employer paid such wages as were necessary to command a supply of the kind of labor he wanted. If he wanted better he paid more; if he paid less he got the leavings and the ineffectives. There were high-wage shops and low-wage shops; also high-wage industries and low-wage industries. In good times wages would rise, as the demand for labor increased; in bad times they would fall, but seldom if ever back to where they were before, because, owing to the mechanization of industry, the productivity of labor was always rising, and for that reason this was a high-wage country, with a rising standard of living, and attracted labor from all over the world.

217

Now wages are determined neither by the employer, as was once said, nor by the law of supply and demand acting in a free labor market, but by the industry-wide bargaining power of an organized and legal labor monopoly.

There was then no intervention by the Federal government in what now we call labor relations, touching the hours of labor, the terms of bargaining between employer and employee, or fixing a minimum wage.

Ford's most celebrated single act was to double the wage rate, not in a gradual manner but by one dramatic stroke. Such a thing had never happened before; it could not happen again. If the law had been then what it now is, and if labor then had been organized as it is today, he would have been haled before the National Labor Relations Board and charged with an unfair labor practice, on the ground that since he did it as an act of his own will and without consulting the labor leaders, his motive could only have been to discredit unionism. Cases of that curious kind are on the record. And certainly, if afterward he had increased the tempo of production in the shop, organized labor would have shut him up.

In that world that is gone the employer controlled the speed of the assembly line. Now labor controls it.

In that world the employer could hire whom he liked and fire whom he disliked, and it was nobody's business. Now a wage earner cannot be fired but for good reason and by consent of the union. The employer must prove his case, and if he fails he will be compelled to rehire the man he fired and pay him wages for the time he was idle. The new way is much more humane, especially as a protection for the weak; the old way is almost forgotten and anyone who speaks of its grim merits will be deemed antisocial.

But most important of all, a man then could do what he would with his profits. Now he has to account for them to the Federal tax collector and share them with the government. The more profit he makes the more of each dollar he must surrender to the government.

The secret of Ford's prodigious achievement lay in what he did with his profits. He shared them with labor by paying high wages, and with his customers by continuously reducing the price of the automobile, and then, but for a relatively small part declared as dividends on the stock, all the rest year after year was returned to the business to buy more and better machines to make more and more automobiles at less and less cost.

But now you have to account to the government for every new machine you buy, and if the tax collector thinks the inefficient old one you threw away was not yet worn out you will have to go on paying taxes on that one besides being taxed on the new one too.

It is easier to imagine other Fords than it is to believe that another would be able to do in this regulated world what Henry Ford did in his free world. He would not be permitted to plow back his profits in that reckless manner as capital; he would not be permitted to parlay his assets out of earnings. He would have to borrow his capital to begin with, instead of creating it as he went along, and his profits on that borrowed capital would be limited—all to the making of a very different story.

Laissez Faire did not survive Henry Ford. It was betrayed by its friends, not for thirty pieces of silver but for debased paper money that would be legal tender for debt. Then it was stoned to death by the multitude and buried with hymns of praise for the easier life.

The obsequies were performed by the government, which assumed at the graveside ultimate responsibility for the continued success, well-being and growth of the national economy; by the government's tax collector, who was to become insatiable, and by organized labor, whose economic power against that of the employer was increased by law, deliberately, on grounds of social policy.

You may like it better this way. Many people do. In any case, it was not to be argued. Only this—that if Laissez Faire had not begotten the richest world that ever existed there would have been much less for the welfare state to distribute.